LIGHTWEIGHT BOATING

Owning and using
expanded polystyrene boats

by
Percy W. Blandford

John Gifford Ltd.
London

© 1970 John Gifford Ltd.

Published by John Gifford Ltd,
            125, Charing Cross Road,
            London, W.C.2.

SBN. 70710012 7

Printed in Great Britain
by Compton Printing Ltd.,
London and Aylesbury

CONTENTS

Chapter 1

ABOUT BOATS

AS far back as history can trace there have been boats. No doubt one of our early ancestors decided it was more comfortable to sit on top of a raft or inside a hollowed log than to sit astride a log with his feet in the water. It would not have been long before he had a paddle of sorts and erected a skin on a mast to let the wind blow him along. For most of the time since, wood has been the commonest boatbuilding material. Iron and steel took over for the largest craft, but not without much shaking of heads and opposition.

In more recent times we have seen plastics in many forms being used for boats and craft of moderate size, so that today at exhibitions and boat shows wooden boats are in a minority. In the last few years the majority of small craft have been glass-reinforced plastic (G.R.P.), more familiarly known to the public as glassfibre, but other plastics have been finding their way into boatbuilding, including expanded polystyrene (conveniently shortened to EPS), which is the reason for this book.

EPS is certainly different from other boatbuilding

materials. In particular, it is cheaper, and this is probably the main reason why many owners have polystyrene craft as their first boats. It has other advantages and disadvantages, so that in discussions it is possible to get bogged down with irrelevancies and side issues. To avoid this, let us start with a few basic principles.

The shape of a boat is more important than the material it is made from, when it comes to performance, and this is the main consideration. If an unballasted boat is to be stable it must have a fairly flattish area of bottom around the centre of the boat (Fig. 1A). Too much of this, however, causes drag, so a floating box may have plenty of initial stability, but its progress through the water would be very sluggish. Plywood cannot be bent in two directions at once, so plywood boats have straight lines in their cross-section, and this shape is called hard chine (Fig. 1B). This is reasonably satisfactory, but the best boat at sea has a rounded bottom, rather like a letter D on edge in its central cross-sections (Fig. 1C).

Another consideration is length. This is a factor affecting speed more than anything else. A long boat is likely to be faster than a short one, even if the other boat has far better lines. As the boat progresses through the water it makes a bow wave, which gets longer as speed increases. When the bow wave is as long as the boat, any increase in power will have very little effect on speed. The longer the boat, the longer bow wave and the greater the speed.

2

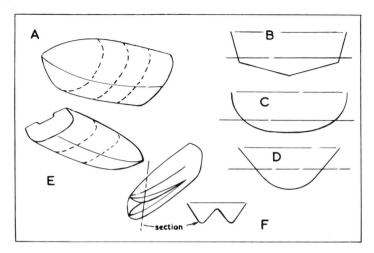

Fig. 1

Then there is skin friction. Smoothness or otherwise of the hull has some effect on this, but more important is the amount of wetted area. The hull form with the minimum wetted area has a semi-circle under water near the centre (Fig. 1D), but as this is very unstable some increase in wetted area to flatten the centre has to be accepted for safety (Fig. 1C).

It is possible to design a hull so that as it reaches a certain speed it begins to rise out of the water and a much smaller area is immersed and causing drag. This is called planing. Most high-powered motor boats and a few racing sailing dinghies plane. The hull has to have a fairly broad and flat bottom most of the way from amidships to the transom (Fig. 1E). With plenty of

3

power it is possible to make a V bottom plane, and this behaves better in broken water at sea. Another way of getting lift is to have a hollow made by twin bows blending into an almost flat stern. This sea sled form (Fig. 1F) forces water and air into the tunnel and this aids lift. With modern materials making many shapes possible which could not have been made easily in wood, much experiment is still going on and a so-called 'cathedral' hull has three bows blending into a flattish transom and two tunnels.

If a boat is to be used for rowing or with a motor, those are the main considerations. If the wind is to be used as the source of power, keel surface has to be provided. This is not to prevent the boat capsizing, as many newcomvers imagine. The occupants of the boat have to act as movable ballast to do that. The keel surface is to give the boat a grip on the water and prevent it blowing sideways when the wind is from the side. If the wind is blowing over the stern, the boat will go ahead and sideways movement will not occur. If the wind is blowing over the bow, sails will flap like flags and the boat will either be stationary or drift backwards, but sideways movement will be no problem. If the wind comes from any other direction the boat will try to go sideways (make leeway) and the keel surface reduces this drift to a minimum.

Keel surface may be central or there can be a keel at each side. There is no strict rule about the disposition of keel surface, so long as there is some. In a small boat the keel surface is usually arranged to pull up into the boat.

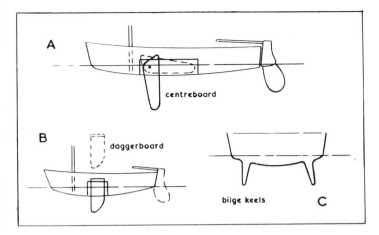

Fig. 2

If it hinges into a case, it is called a centreboard (Fig. 2A). If it lifts up and down, it is a daggerboard (Fig. 2B). If there are twin keels (bilge keels), they may lift into the boat, but more likely they are permanently in place (Fig. 2C). The boat can rest on them when ashore. The sailing boat also needs a rudder. Besides its obvious use in steering, it is deep enough to help the keel in preventing leeway. A rudder for a rowing boat can be much shallower.

If a square sail is hung from a yard on the mast, the boat will sail away from the wind (running) and can progress at an angle each side of directly down wind, but it is unlikely to sail at right-angles to the wind (reaching) or make any progress towards it (tacking, beating or close-hauled). Square-rigged sailing ships, having little windward ability, had to wait for the wind or follow routes where the winds were known to be mostly favourable (trade winds).

Modern small craft have fore-and-aft rigs and nearly all are sloops. A sloop has a single mast, with a main sail aft of it and a smaller sail forward of it, strictly a 'foresail' but today more often called a 'jib'. The jib is always triangular but the main sail can be a variety of shapes. A racing dinghy nearly always has a Bermudan main sail (Fig. 3A). This is triangular, with a tall mast and is the most efficient rig to windward, but the long mast is sometimes a problem in stowage or transport. An alternative of very similar final shape is the gunter rig (Fig. 3B). All of the spars can then be as short as the boat. In a very small boat one way of getting sufficient sail area without long spars is to have a sprit sail (Fig. 3C). On a much bigger scale this is seen in the traditional Thames barge.

How does polystyrene, as a constructional material, fit into the boating pattern and match up with other boatbuilding materials? Although it is not impossible to shape a block of EPS by hand, this is not the method used for building boats. The method of building boats or anything else in quantity from the material requires a sufficient demand to justify expensive machinery to turn out identical hulls at comparatively high speed. When the demand is sufficient a large number can be produced to spread the original cost, the price of an individual boat can be kept quite low.

Once the shape has been settled it has to be accepted

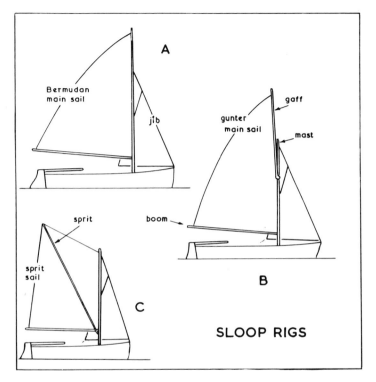

Fig. 3

as modifications would be expensive. EPS can be made into any shape, within reason, so it allows for new ideas being applied to boat forms. Some EPS hulls differ little from what may be considered the conventional shapes developed for other materials. Others have shapes, fins, keels and other specialities that would be difficult or

7

impossible in most other materials. Consequently, we are in the hands of the designer, who has used his skill and experience to take advantage of the possibilities of EPS, sometimes to incorporate ideas which have not previously been tried. Such is progress and only time will tell if a new idea is the great success the designer expects.

EPS as used for boats is of much higher density than the polystyrene used for packaging and other purposes. Even so, it is still quite soft compared with wood and GRP. It has little strength, so it has to be used in a much greater thickness than the other materials. Normal thicknesses are around 2in. and will be more at points of special load. Surfaces are easily damaged by impact, so an EPS dinghy is almost bound to suffer in appearance as it is used, unless extreme care is taken. While repairs are possible and paint will freshen up appearance, a battered appearance of some degree must be accepted. Priced in the gleam of varnish and the smoothness of hull surfaces is not for the EPS boat owner — at least not as regards the hull.

EPS is extremely buoyant. This means that the boat itself will float whatever happens to it. Filling with water will have little effect on flotation. Holing or even breaking up into little pieces will not sink it. Although this means that the boat will never sink under you and you do not have to use up space inside with buoyancy compartments or air bags, the great buoyancy means the boat floats very high and this brings its own problems, which are discussed in the next chapter.

Polystyrene is affected by heat and many solvents. A flame causes it to disappear rather than burn or dissolve. The solvents used in many adhesives dissolve it. Petrol and oil dissolve it — perhaps not rapidly, but at a rate sufficient for precautions to be necessary.

Chapter 2

EPS BOATMANSHIP

SEAMANSHIP is an all-embracing term which it is difficult to define. A competent seaman is one who appreciates the element in which he is working, who knows how to handle his craft efficiently and safely, who has already planned what he would do in an emergency and who knows what he can and cannot do with his craft. Seamanship is a term usually related to large craft. Boatmanship is a better term for small boats and it can embrace inland as well as sea boating. The competent boatman should take a pride in all the seamanlike attributes as they would be related to his smaller command.

Safety of boat and crew should be a first consideration. Ideally, anyone who goes afloat in water too deep to walk out of, should be able to swim — 50 yards is often quoted as the desirable distance, but what is important is the freedom from panic which the ability to swim gives in the event of an unexpected ducking. Usually there is no need to swim any great distance as the best advice is always to stay with the boat.

If non-swimmers are taken afloat they should wear a

lifejacket or buoyancy aid. On open waters and when sailing swimmers should do the same. This is customary and many clubs insist on the practice. If you know that you will remain afloat without having to go through the motions of swimming, you can give your attention to other things, such as righting the boat.

In Britain 'lifejacket' and 'buoyancy aid' have different meanings. Lifejackets which are approved by the British Standards Institute are capable of bringing the wearer to the surface and turning him on his back with his mouth well above the water in a very short time, even if he is unconscious. Most of these lifejackets have permanent buoyancy in the form of closed cell plastic foam and can be given additional buoyancy by mouth inflation. The greatest bulk of permanent buoyancy material is in front and there is more around the collar.

A lifejacket is necessarily bulky and as boatmen might be discouraged from wearing one constantly the Ship and Boat Builders National Federation approve a buoyancy aid which is able to keep its wearer afloat, but not necessarily the right way up. If the wearer is conscious he can float upright without difficulty. Most buoyancy aids are like waistcoats with the buoyant material fairly evenly spread around them, to keep the bulk low and the aid is not much more than an additional garment which does not interfere with activity.

Obviously there is a case for the greater safety of a lifejacket, particularly on open waters, but a buoyancy aid may be acceptable on more restricted waters if you think the risk of being knocked unconscious is remote. The swinging boom of a sailing dinghy has been known to deliver a knock-out blow.

For personal safety in regard to the boat, EPS craft present a special problem because of their considerable buoyancy, which makes them sit on top of the water rather than penetrate into it by an appreciable amount. This means that air movements have more effect than water movements. In anything of a wind the boat, regardless of sails, can travel quite fast over the surface before the wind, without allowing for any movement of the water. This could mean that a light person might not give the boat much grip on the water and attempts to row might not be good enough to propel the boat to windward. The problem with children is then something akin to the use of air mattresses. In an offshore wind, they might blow out to sea and their own efforts would not be good enough to get back. This means that in open waters a child should not be left to handle an EPS boat in conditions where the wind is blowing away from the place where he has to return.

The great buoyancy is also a problem if the boat capsizes. Dealing with a capsize is dealt with later, but from a safety point of view the important rule is to always stay with the boat. This means hanging on to something when you go over. If you are separated from the boat and there is much wind, the hull floats so high that the wind will carry it along at a speed too great for any swimmer to overhaul. If your boat capsizes and you

The Mailboat spritsail rig is distinctive and gets the sail area high without having a very tall mast.

The buoyancy of EPS can be seen in the way the Mailboat, with its EPS

are unable to deal with the incident yourself and have to be rescued, the boat is much more easily seen from a distance than a bobbing head amongst the waves. If gear floats away, do not be tempted to swim after it unless you retain some connection with the boat, possibly by a rope.

Another thing the real boatman does is check on the boat's equipment. He does not push off and discover that some vital thing is left ashore. To a certain extent details depend on particular boats. There should always be a second means of propulsion. If the wind dies on you, how do you get back? If the outboard motor fails, can you get to safety? On a lake or river, a sailing dinghy can be propelled by a paddle or even the dagger board. On more open waters, oars and rowlocks are needed. These can also be the second method for a motor boat.

Even the smallest boat should have a bow painter. This is a good length of rope firmly secured somewhere in the bows and used for mooring the boat or taking a tow. A piece of Terylene about ¾in. circumference and 10ft. long will suit most small boats. Do not be tempted to economise by using discarded clothes line or other doubtful rope. It is a help to have a second similar rope at the stern. You can then moor or hold the boat alongside a bank.

If the boat is only being used for rowing, the oars should be in sound condition and the rowlocks should be retained in some way. In some types their design makes them secure against accidental removal. If they are the normal type, there should be a lanyard of light line tied or spliced around their neck and the other end fastened to something in the boat (Fig. 4A).

If a rowlock is lost overboard you could be in a dangerous situation. Sculling over the stern is a possible alternative with one oar. This is not as fast and is more applicable to finding your way through a crowded anchorage, but it will get you home. In a traditional wooden boat there may be a notch in the transom for sculling, but it may be possible to fit an extra rowlock socket on a wood block on the transom and use that. Instructions on rowing and sculling are given later.

If the boat is to be sailed, it is usually wiser to completely rig it before leaving the shore. You are not likely then to leave anything important behind. In some circumstances it is necessary to lower the main sail while you paddle or row off, but the preliminary rigging makes sure all is right and avoids unnecessary standing, which can be dangerous in a small boat floating uncontrolled, as it will be for a brief period.

If you are to use an outboard motor, a safety precaution is to have a line from the motor to a strong point in the boat, so that the motor cannot jump off. Every year a large number of motors are lost in this way. If it is a small motor, quite a light rope will do, but for a powerful motor it is better to have flexible wire or chain.

Except when going in very restricted waters, it is unwise to go afloat with a motor without a few tools and a spare plug. Obviously there should be adequate

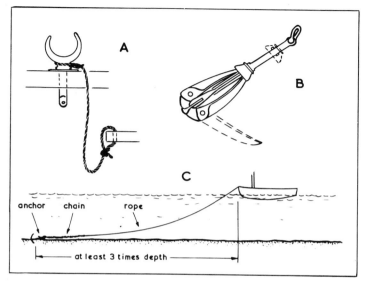

Fig. 4

fuel, mixed ashore.

An anchor is often advocated for small boats. One will certainly stop you drifting away with the tide or prevent you running down on to a river weir. The snag with a small EPS boat is stowing the anchor and its cable. For most boating done in these craft an anchor is unnecessary. Most anchors are spiky and liable to damage both the crew and the EPS boat, unless a wood sheath or other stowage is arranged. There is a type of folding grapnel which is particularly suitable for these boats as the four points are covered when folded

(Fig. 4B). One of these, weighing 3lb., with a few feet of chain, followed by perhaps 50ft. of ¾in. Terylene rope, does not take up much stowage space and will do a proper anchoring job when required.

The technique of anchoring is to face up into the current or wind, whichever is stronger, then lower the anchor, not throw it, over the bow. After it has touched bottom the boat goes astern until at least three times as much cable has been let out. By then you should be able to feel the anchor biting and you can make the cable fast to a cleat. Of course, the end of the cable should have already been secured to prevent the lot going overboard. An anchor holds by its pull along the bottom, not by its dead weight. With a small anchor the length of chain next to it helps to keep the pull low (Fig. 4C).

Any boatman should know a few knots. The common knot for a temporary mooring is a clove hitch. Over a post, two similar loops are formed (Fig. 5A) and dropped on to the end. If it is a ring or somewhere where the end is not available, the end is taken around and over the rope from the boat (Fig. 5B), then continued around the same way and under itself (Fig. 5C) to get the same result. A better and more permanent knot for the end of a rope is the round turn and two half hitches (Fig. 5D). In this the end first completely encircles the object (Fig. 5E), then the standing part is kept straight and the end used to make a clove hitch around it (Fig. 5F) to complete the knot. For greater permanency, as at the end of the anchor

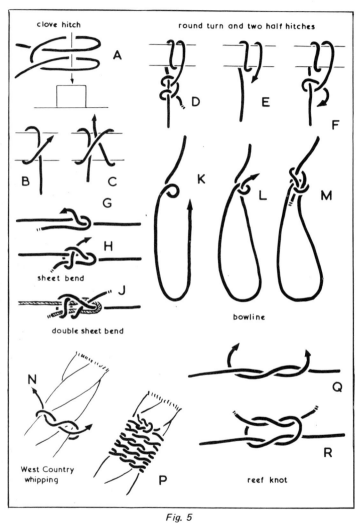

clove hitch

round turn and two half hitches

A

B C

G

D E F

K L M

sheet bend

H

double sheet bend

J

bowline

West Country whipping

N

P

Q

reef knot

R

Fig. 5

cable, the end may be seized down with light line.

The general joining knot is the sheet bend, whether the ropes are the same or different thicknesses. Bend one end back on itself (the thicker if there is a difference) and pass the other end up through this loop (Fig. 5G). Take it around behind the loop and across under itself (Fig. 5H). If there is much difference between the thickness or the ropes are slippery, go around a second time to make a double sheet bend (Fig. 5J).

The knot for a loop in the end of a rope is a bowline. The actual crossing is similar to a sheet bend. Take a length sufficient for the loop and make a small eye (Fig. 5K). Bring the end through this, going in at the same side as the standing part (Fig. 5L). Hold the eye in shape with one hand while taking the end around the standing part and down through the loop (Fig. 5M). This completes the form of the knot, but be careful not to pull it out of shape when tightening.

Most ropes used afloat today are synthetic. They have a much longer life than natural fibre ropes, which soon rot. Terylene is most popular. Nylon has more stretch. Other synthetic ropes are cheaper and mostly not as strong, but new rope materials frequently appear and it is not easy to keep up with developments. Nearly all synthetic ropes can have their ends sealed by heating. With a cigarette lighter rather than a match (which is sooty) heat the rope end while it is being turned slowly. Moisten a finger and thumb and roll the end so that the molten end blends into a solid mass. This is probably secure against unlaying, but it is more seamanlike to also apply a whipping.

Terylene whipping line is obtainable and a West Country whipping is simple and effective for all ropes. With a short piece of whipping line, knot it near the centre around the rope (Fig. 5N). Take the ends behind and knot again. Continue along the rope, pulling tight each time you knot back and front. Cover a length about the same as the thickness of the rope and finish with a reef knot (Fig. 5P).

A reef knot is not the general-purpose joining knot, as some people assume. It is only safe when bearing against something, as it did when used for the reef points of sails. It is made by twisting the two ends together one way (Fig. 5Q) and then the other way (Fig. 5R) so that the ends come out alongside the standing parts. If they come out across the knot, the second twist was the wrong way and the result is a useless granny knot.

The load which most EPS boats will carry is considerable. This does not mean it is wise to carry anything like the maximum load. The direct load that would push a boat under is probably more than could be got into the boat, whatever common material is used, but a heavily loaded boat need only list a little way for it to become unstable and deposit its load in the water.

The maximum wise load should be known. There is a proper way to load a boat. Beginners tend to step on to gunwales or thwarts. They may get away with it, or they may find themselves in the water. Whenever possible, the foot should go right into the bottom of the boat, as near central as possible. The load should be distributed properly. It is better to be slightly down at the stern than at the bow. If the boat is being rowed, the oarsman will soon start complaining if the boat is wrongly trimmed. Be careful when unloading. If the central oarsman gets out and leaves only a heavy passenger in the stern of a small boat, the boat could tilt at an alarming angle, if nothing worse happens.

A boatman should also be aware of the effects of wind, tide and current. The boat is supported on water which may be moving and then at different speeds at different places or times. There may be a considerable rise and fall of tides. Above the water, the wind may affect the boat. These effects have to be weighed up against each other and acted upon. More information on wind and tide is given elsewhere in the book.

A capable boatman understands what he should do in relation to other craft. There are most comprehensive rules for preventing collisions at sea. If you dive straight into them, you will merely become bewildered. For a start remember that power (including rowing) boats give way to sailing craft. If you meet another boat head on and there would be a collision if you did nothing about it, you alter course so as to pass port to port (keep to the right when passing).

Large commercial craft have to keep to deep channels and cannot alter course very quickly and may take several miles to stop. Small pleasure craft obviously keep out of their way. Do not try to exercise right of sail over power when meeting a cargo vessel in the

Thames Estuary, for instance.

An overtaking boat keeps out of the way of one being overtaken and the overtaken boat maintains its course until the other has passed, whether either or both are sail or power. If you are under power and arrive at a sailing race which just about fills the river, it would obviously be unfair to expect all river traffic to stop for the duration of the race. On most rivers it is the accepted thing for power craft to creep by slowly close to one bank. It is usually possible to time things so that you pass under the stern of a sailing boat just after it has tacked.

The rules between one sailing boat and another are a little more complex and if racing you will have to become familiar with a great many, but for general sailing you can cope with most situations if you remember that when two sailing craft are meeting on different tacks, the one on starboard tack (main sail out to port) has right of way. If both are on the same tack the one to leeward (downwind) has right of way.

There are accepted sound signals you should know about. You may not use them, but a tug skipper or other commercial boatman may use them and assume you understand. A horn blast does not necessarily mean 'Get out of my so-and-so way', although a series of short blasts mean something like that. A single short blast means 'I am altering my course to starboard' (his right). It could mean that if you are meeting head on, he is preparing to pass you port to port, and expects you to do the same. Two short blasts mean 'I am altering my course to port'. This may be to go alongside a wharf and he is expecting you to understand and keep out of the way. Three short blasts mean 'My engines are going astern'. This does not necessarily mean he is going backwards. There are no brakes on a boat and reversing is the only way of slowing and stopping. Four short blasts followed by one after an interval means 'I am going about to starboard'. The boat is turning right round to the right. If the four blasts are followed by two, the boat is going about to port.

Chapter 3

OARS AND POWER

ROWING is not difficult, but an EPS boat needs a special technique. As the boat is so light and mostly above the water you will make best progress by using short sharp strokes. This is particularly so if you are rowing in waves. If you try to use long strokes, the boat will lose way between strokes. If there is a cross-wind you will have difficulty in maintaining your course.

Sit squarely on the centre thwart facing aft. If it is possible to brace your feet against something, do so, otherwise try to get a grip with your soles flat on the bottom of the boat. When you put power into your pulling you will find you press quite hard on your feet. If the rowlocks have uneven sides, have the higher side forward so that they take the thrust of the oar as you pull. If the oars have leathers, see that these are in the rowlocks. If the oars match the boat, the grips should come within a few inches of each other (Fig. 6A).

You have to get used to your view being of where you have come from rather than where you are going. If you are alone you may have to glance over your shoulder occasionally to check on your course. If you

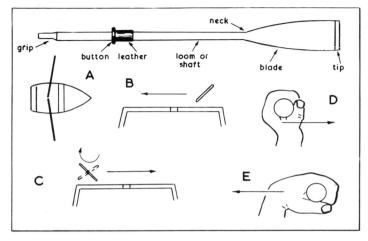

Fig. 6

are lucky, there will be a couple of marks somewhere astern which you can keep in the same relation to each other as a check that you are on course. If you have a mate sitting in the stern, he can tell you any course corrections. If you are new to rowing, the boat will wander (yaw) quite a lot, but your course-keeping should improve with a little practice.

The snag with a small buoyant boat is that its shape offers little aid to keeping on course. It wants to pivot at a point somewhere near its centre. Fixed keels help, but their greatest area is in the region of the point where the boat pivots, so their effect is not as great as might be expected. Of course, a rudder is a help. Your mate can steer, but he should apply corrections when the oars are out of the water, otherwise he increases your work. If you have to row a short dinghy alone some way, it might be worthwhile fitting the rudder and lashing the tiller centrally, so that the rudder blade acts as a skeg and keeps the boat straight.

Steering by the oars is by pulling harder one side or the other. You can turn on the spot by pulling on one side and backwatering on the other. The river oarsman, in his long slim boat, takes long strokes and feathers the blades parallel with the water when they are in the air. This is done by dipping the wrists when pushing forward. With the short sharp strokes in a fairly tubby dinghy there is no time for feathering. Your performance may look like a windmill, but it is the most effective way in these boats. Aim to get the blades just immersed — there is nothing to gain by dipping them too deeply. Return with the blades clear of the water, but no higher than necessary.

The word 'sculling' on a river means pulling with a pair of oars and 'rowing' is reserved for one oar per man. On the coast, 'rowing' is with one or a pair of oars and 'sculling' is using one oar over the stern. Sculling over the stern is not as difficult as it appears. Bystanders are always impressed when you bring your boat in by waggling one oar over the transom.

The important thing to remember is what is happening under the water. The blade is drawn across at about 45 degrees to the direction it is going (Fig. 6B). At the end of the stroke it is turned so that the same side is aft and taken back the other way, still at about

45 degrees (Fig. 6C). The effect of this is to try to push the boat both sideways and forward, but because of the shape of the bottom of the boat, most of the result is in forward motion and the reversing of the strokes cancels out much of the sideways motion. Even then the stern of a small light boat slews from side to side noticably.

The twist is obtained by a wrist action. If you bend your wrist as far forward and backwards as it will go, the movement is about 90 degrees. The oar is pulled across with the wrist bent back (Fig. 6D). At the end of that stroke, it is bent forward to twist the blade to the new direction (Fig. 6E) and taken across to the other side. This can be done while standing or sitting sideways and looking forward. The other hand can be used to help pull, but control should be by the one wrist. Sculling can be rather hard on untried wrist muscles, but it is a useful way of moving your boat in confined spaces, getting up narrow creeks and seeing where you are going.

Power

AN outboard motor is a self-contained power unit intended to cramp on to the transom. When it drives, it can put quite a twisting strain across the transom. Consequently an outboard motor should only be used on an EPS boat if the makers have strengthened the transom to take it, and then a motor of no greater power than that recommended. Most small boats intended primarily for rowing or sailing, do not have a hull shape that would take advantage of a high-powered motor, so nothing is to be gained by overpowering. Such a boat up to about 12ft. does not need more than 3 HP and in most circumstances half this power would be sufficient.

If the hull is designed for planing, it will not be at its best when off the plane. It is not as good a sea boat at low speeds as one designed for low power. To get an average runabout type on to a plane needs at least 10 HP with perhaps one on board. Something nearer .double that is needed for four or is the absolute minimum for water-ski-ing. The makers will usually specify the maximum power they expect their boat to take. It is important that the motor and its propeller are matched to the boat, if the best results are to be obtained, although most motors have propellers designed to suit average boats intended to take their power.

Nearly all outboard motors are two-strokes. The smaller ones have single cylinders. Larger motors have two or more. The small motors, up to about 5 HP, may have a fuel tank mounted on the motor. Larger motors have a separate tank which stands in the boat and is connected to the motor by a flexible hose. Nearly all the motors for boats of the size we are considering, are started by pulling a cord, either a loose one around a flanged pulley or an enclosed recoil type. Larger motors may have electric starting.

Outboard motors are normally available to suit two heights of transom. The standard motor is for a 15in. transom, measured from under the mounting bracket to the bottom of the hull. Longshaft motors are for 20in.

transoms. Other lengths would be to special order only. Using a motor of insufficient length means that the propeller does not receive a flow of undisturbed water and does not perform efficiently. Most small boats suit a standard length motor, but the Mailboat is one that is well up to the limit for a longshaft motor.

If the propeller hits anything solid while running, the shock transmitted through to the power head could do damage if there was no safety precaution. Most motors have the propeller driven through a shear pin. This breaks and prevents damage to more important parts. If the retaining nut is removed from the propeller shaft, the propeller will slide off and the shear pin can be seen. A few spares should be carried. The popular British Seagull motors use a spring instead of a shear pin. This takes some shock, but may break and a spare should be carried.

The makers specify the type of oil to use and the proportion to mix with the petrol. Care is needed to measure correctly. Slap-happy guessing can lead to trouble. Two-stroke mixture as supplied for scooters is in the wrong proportion for most outboard motors.

As petrol and oil attack polystyrene, the makers may have provided a certain amount of protection in the area where the motor will be. There may be sheet plastic or there may be a coating of protective paint or sheathing. It is still important to keep petrol and oil away from the boat as much as possible. Mixing and filling should be done ashore. If fuel has to be carried for topping up on a long trip, a can with a built-in pourer is best. Using a

This view of a Pioneer shows that the hull shape is very similar to conventional dinghies.

One of the prototype TV dinghies being tried out at Hayling Island. The full length batten in the main sail gives increased area without carrying the

can and a funnel is almost certainly bound to mean some fuel going where it should not. Any spilled mixture should be wiped off polystyrene and the area washed with water. Apart from the risk of damage to the boat, some inland waters have regulations concerning the spillage of fuel in the water.

Do not carry spare fuel in large cans. It is much easier to handle a small can with a spout when afloat. So that there can be no risk of damage to the hull, any cans and the remote tank for a large motor should be kept on board in polythene bags if there is no specially proofed mounting.

Starting drill is quite simple. If there is a clutch, put it in neutral. Close the choke. Open the air vent of the fuel tank, turn on the fuel if it is a gravity tank on the motor, or pump up fuel from a remote tank — usually by squeezing a bulb. Set the throttle as recommended by the makers — usually about one-third open. Pull the starter cord. The motor should start after about three pulls. If it does, most motors require the choke opening almost immediately. To stop the motor, some have a button to press, while others stop when throttled fully back.

Larger motors have a gear lever. There are no gears, as on a car, but this lever can be set at forward, neutral and reverse. This means that when you have started the motor you have time in neutral while you cast off from the bank and get ready to go. Small motors are without a clutch, which means the propeller is driving as soon as the motor starts. If you have a mate, he can hold on to the bank and resist the low-speed drive of the motor, while you prepare to go. If you are alone, you have to arrange the painter so that you can let go quickly and have everything ready for you to sit down and be under way as the boat moves forward immediately.

There is no separate rudder with an outboard motor and steering is by the drive of the propeller, controlled by a tiller on the motor, which usually carries the throttle. Small motors are arranged so that they turn completely in their mounting. This means that the motor can be turned right round to drive astern. Steering by the thrust of the motor is very positive, but once the motor is shut off, your steering has gone.

As steering is by the thrust of the motor, the turning point of the boat comes further aft than when it is rowed. This means that moving the tiller to turn the boat tends to thrust the stern of the boat sidways and this may have to be allowed for. It may be a problem when getting away from a bank. With the boat parallel with the bank, turning the motor with the intention of driving the bow out causes the corner of the transom to bump along the bank (Fig. 7A). It may be better to reverse the motor and draw the stern away (Fig. 7B), then bring the boat into the direction you want to go and change to forward gear (Fig. 7C).

If there is any current, it is usual to start and finish with the boat pointing against the stream, unless there is a strong wind blowing the opposite way, when it might be better to head into that. By doing this, the wind or stream has a braking effect. Coming in the other way,

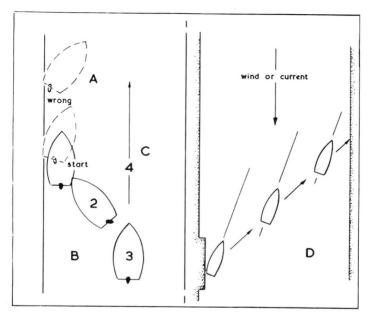

Fig. 7

with stream and motor driving the same way, will probably mean some undignified grabbing of the bank in an attempt to stop as you sweep past. With the current (or wind) against the motor, you have a brake effect.

If there is very much stream or a very high wind, and you want to cross at an angle to it, your actual course will be widely different from the way you are heading, and this will have to be allowed for. The current (or wind) will cause you to go crabwise and you will have to keep the boat headed slightly upstream of your destination to allow for this (Fig. 7D). Only experience will show you how much to allow.

Fuel consumption of an outboard motor can be rather high. The smallest seem economical enough, but large motors on planing hulls use fuel rapidly if kept fully opened. In fact having the throttle three-quarters open instead of fully open can cut fuel consumption to half, so there is some advantage in running costs in having a motor slightly more powerful than might be needed normally and running it throttled back.

There are few four-stroke outboard motors, particularly in the lower powers. They use straight petrol in the tank and have oil in a sump. They are not so likely to oil up plugs. If a two-stroke motor stops and will not restart, changing the plug will quite often make a cure. A spare plug and its spanner should normally be taken afloat.

There are electric outboard motors, but all of quite low power. The largest is about ¾ HP and will drive a small boat at a moderate speed on placid inland waters for about 6 hours on one charge of a car battery. The motor is immediately ahead of the propeller and only a variable speed control and a tiller come above the water. These motors are absolutely quiet and useful for bird watching or trolling when fishing. For an EPS boat they have the advantage of not needing petrol or anything else that will attack the material.

If a two-stroke outboard motor fails to start or

otherwise gives trouble, the remedy is usually fairly simple. At one time outboard motors had a reputation for being temperamental, but modern ones are normally very reliable. Providing the motor gets fuel in the right proportion and a spark at the right time, it should function. If fuel is gravity-fed allow time for the carburettor to fill before starting. If the carburettor has a 'tickler', this can be used to check when the float chamber is full. With most motors the starter cord has to be pulled quite sharply to spin the magneto at a high enough speed to give a good spark. If the motor fails to start after several pulls there is a risk of an excessive amount of fuel in the cylinder and the spark plug points becoming wet so that they will not spark. If this is suspected, open the throttle and choke wide, then give several pulls to blow out the excess fuel. It is possible the motor may start while you are doing this. If so, quickly re-adjust the throttle. More likely, nothing will happen. Wait a minute or so, to allow the wet plug to dry out, then try a normal start again.

If a motor gives trouble and there is no obvious fault, changing the plug is the first thing to try. It is possible to test if a plug is sparking by removing it, then fix its wire again and hold it so that its body is earthed against a part of the motor, while the starting cord is pulled. Shade the plug, otherwise the spark may not be seen in bright sunlight, and be careful to hold the plug so that you do not get a shock from the wire or terminal. If the normal waterproof cover is used, this should be no problem.

Maintenance of the average outboard motor is slight. Although it might not be a case of thriving on neglect, it is a fact that many people continue to use outboard motors season after season without bothering much about them between times. If a motor is water-cooled it is unwise to ever tilt it so that the underwater gear is higher than the power head. Water trapped inside might run into places where it should not be. When the motor is removed from the transom, keep it upright long enough for most of the water to drain out, in any case. The bottom assembly is lubricated by grease or oil, and it is important that this is kept filled, according to the makers' instructions and with the recommended lubricant. Elsewhere there is little lubrication needed. It is certainly unwise to be too enthusiastic about lubricating in the vicinity of electrical gear. For prolonged storage the makers usually recommend squirting some oil through the plug hole, and turning the engine over occasionally during storage.

Most modern motors are made of seawater-resistant metals. Evenso, it is a good idea to run a motor in fresh water after sea use to reduce the risk of salt deposits building up. If a motor is to be stored, it is a good idea to wash it off and remove any dirty oil deposits from spilt mixture with petrol, then wipe over with a cloth soaked in a light oil.

For a motor to be used on an EPS hull, where fuel and oil could attack the hull, cleanliness of the motor should be considered even more important than when used elsewhere. It is advisable to keep the motor on the transom until it can be lifted ashore, but if it has to be removed and carried in the boat, the only leakage of fuel that might be expected is from the carburettor when the motor is put on its side. If the tank is on the motor, the air vent is screwed down and the tap in the pipeline turned off. This seals the supply, but some of the small amount in the carburettor may trickle out when the motor is on its side. If the motor is to be regularly carried on its side in the boat it might be as well to experiment to find which way produces least leakage and have a tray to put under the dripping location. In emergency, a cloth to absorb the drips, over plastic sheeting will protect the boat. Some carburettors have a drain point under the float chamber. If this is opened before removing the motor from the transom there should be no spillage problem. If the motor is cold, the power head can be wrapped in a polythene bag.

Heat affects EPS so the motor should be left on the transom to cool before being removed and laid in the boat. If it has to be put in the boat soon after stopping see that the silencer and other hot parts of the exhaust system do not come next to the hull. The heat may also be sufficient to char wood or damage other materials.

The efficiency of an outboard motor is affected by the way it is mounted on a boat. It is the boat/motor combination which should be considered. The motor should be mounted so that it drives as near as possible parallel with the surface. The boat progresses at its best speed if it is as near horizontal as possible. A common sight is a lone man sitting close against the transom, with the bow high in the air (Fig. 8A). The effective length of the boat is only that part immersed and speed is reduced accordingly. It would be better for the helmsman to get near the centre of the boat (Fig. 8B), but with many motors this means rather a long stretch to control the short tiller. It is possible to get extension tillers for some motors. If there are two or more people in the boat it is easier to trim to get the best performance.

The angles of boat transoms vary, so motors are provided with an angle adjustment on their mounting brackets. In recent years the transom angle on most boats intended for an outboard motor have been made at 10 − 15 degrees to the vertical, but angles can vary tremendously. A little experiment with the boat under way and normally loaded will show the best angle to set the motor. Even with a large motor on a boat intended to plane, the final attitude of the boat should not be very far off horizontal, and when the boat is in the planing position the thrust of the propeller should be parallel with the surface of the water.

Besides the angle adjustment for driving, many motors also have a lock to hold the motor at an angle which brings the underwater gear above the surface. In some cases it is a frictional arrangement, but a strut is more common. With this it is possible to leave the motor mounted in place, but clear of the water, so that it does not cause drag, while the boat is rowed or sailed. It then has to be mounted to one side of the transom, to

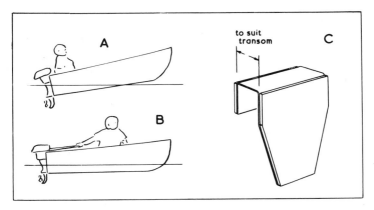

Fig. 8

give the rudder room to move. Most motors can have the steering locked to drive forward. You can then, if you wish, steer with the boat's rudder.

Most mounting brackets have one or two clamping screws with large washerlike ends, and these mark the transom. For some motors there are plastic pads to fix to the transom to take the screw ends. A further advantage is that the pads positively locate the motor. An alternative is to hinge two pieces of plywood on a piece of rubberized or plastic fabric to hang over the transom (Fig. 8C). The piece outside should be large enought ot take the whole of the bracket, as this is where the thrust comes. The length of the hinge fabric should suit the thickness of the transom so that the edges of the plywood come near the top.

Chapter 4

SAILING

FOR most people the greatest joy of owning a small boat is in sailing it. Much of the fascination in sailing any boat is the fact that the rudiments of sailing are soon learned, and a beginner can go afloat and soon make the boat go where he wants, yet it is always possible to improve technique and the enthusiast of many years experience is still learning and finding ways to make his boat go faster or point higher into the wind. In this mechanical age there is also the great satisfaction to be got from harnessing the wind and using it to drive the boat the way you want to go.

One ship goes east one ship goes west
By the self-same wind that blows,
But it is the set of the sails and not the gales
That determine the way she goes.'

This may be a rather awful bit of doggerel, but it does show that it is the angle of the sails that control the direction of the boat.

There are more than enough sailing terms. Many of them date from the days before power craft and are related to large sailing ships. Some of the terms have no

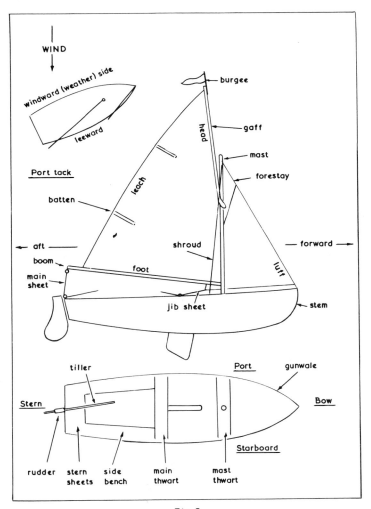

Fig. 9

relevant applications to small boat sailing and are better regarded only as historically interesting, but that does not stop some people trying to air their nautical knowledge and mystify newcomers. It is better to use commonsense and employ everyday words until the few essential terms come of their own accord. Some words are used as we progress through this chapter, while others will be found in the glossary.

Many sailing terms (Fig. 9) are related to the direction of the wind. The left side, when facing forward, may still be *port*, and the right side *starboard*, but the direction the wind is coming from is *windward* and that side of the boat is the *weather* side. The opposite direction is *leeward* (pronounced 'looard') and it is the *lee* side. If the wind is coming over the stern, for purposes of direction, the sides the sails are is the leeward side.

The average boat with a modern rig can be sailed in any direction except within about 45 degrees of directly into the wind (Fig. 10A). A racing boat with a tall Bermudan mast may get rather closer to the wind, but a knockabout dinghy with a modest rig will only progress at a rather wider angle.

A boat sailing as close as it is able towards the wind is *close-hauled* (Fig. 10B). If it is sailing at right-angles to the wind it is *reaching* (Fig. 10C). This is the easiest direction to sail a boat, and sailors call a beam wind a 'soliders' wind', implying that even they could sail a boat that way. When the wind is aft the boat is *running* (Fig. 10D).

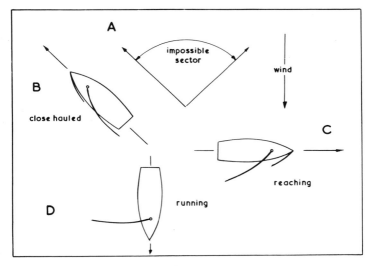

Fig. 10

Ropes which raise or lower sails, flags or anything else are called *halyards* (also spelled *halliards).* Ropes that control sails are called *sheets.* Ropes (usually wire) which support the mast are collectively called *standing rigging.* Sheets and halyards are *running rigging.* In a small boat the mast may stand without rigging, but if there is any, the stay going forward to the stem, or near it, is the *forestay,* while those going each side to the *gunwales* (pronounced 'gunnels') are *shrouds.* If there is a spar at the top of a sail it is a *gaff* if it is wholly aft of the mast. If it crosses the mast it is a *yard.*

A pulley wheel over which a rope runs is called a

sheave. If the sheave is in a case it is called a *block*. An eye on the block is a *becket*. A fitting to which a rope is *made fast* is a *cleat*, although a large one for mooring is a *bollard*. A fitting through which a rope is led is called a *fairlead*. Seats across the boat are *thwarts*. Those along the side are side *benches*. Seating in the stern is *stern sheets* (with an 's).

Much of the skill in sailing is in setting the sails by experience and instinct. The behaviour of the boat, the attitude it takes up, the direction it heads, the feel on the tiller and many other things tell the experienced helmsman whether to pay out or haul in his sheet. The beginner has to start somewhere and it may be a help to regard sail setting as a piece of geometry. When you get afloat, the wind does not come at you in the form of arrows on a diagram and it·is sometimes rather fickle so that it varies over quite a wide arc, but we have to make a start and a little paperwork helps.

You have the boat broadside to the wind and you want to sail in that direction. Imagine a line representing the wind through the mast and another representing direction through the centreline of the boat. Bisecting the angle between these lines gives you the angle of the sail (Fig. 11A). This holds whatever the angle. If you want to sail close-hauled, the angle between the lines gets less, so the bisected angle is less and the sail is hauled in closer to the boat (Fig. 11B). If you sail off the wind the angle gets wider and the sail goes farther out (Fig. 11C). Of course, a point is reached where the lines representing the wind direction and the boat

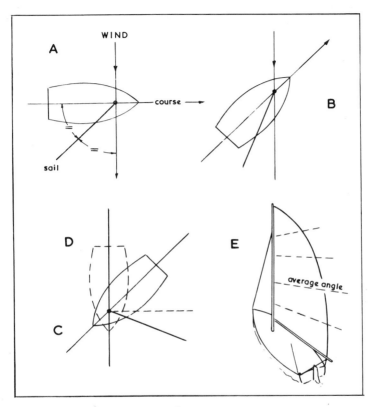

Fig. 11

direction coincide and the sail goes out at right-angles to them (Fig. 11D).

This is theory and would be just about correct, if the sail was a flat board. Instead, it is a flexible cloth, which goes out at a much greater angle at the top than it does where it is held by the sheet at the bottom, so the theoretical angle must be regarded as the average one. In a racing boat the sail may be kept as near as possible to the same angle by long battens and by hauling down with a kicking strap or a central sheet arrangement, but in a general-purpose dinghy the top of the sail falls off quite a long way in relation to the bottom. This means in practice that the bottom of the sail has to be hauled in much farther than the theoretical average angle (Fig. 11E).

It is convenient to learn to sail in a una-rigged boat (one with a single sail), although if there is a jib, it is set at the same angle as the main sail most of the time. If you wish to sail to windward, you haul in the main sail almost as far as it will come. You may use the rudder to get the boat pointing the right way, but for most sailing it is the sail position that steers as well as drives. Once you are on course and sailing the tiller will be near central. Normally the helmsman sits to windward, with one hand on the tiller and the other holding the main sheet (Fig. 12A). How far you sit up to windward depends on the strength of the wind. If you have a crew, his main job is as movable ballast. Besides keeping your boat near upright, you have to dispose your weight so that it trims properly in a fore and aft direction. At first it is useful to have someone ashore observing the boat and advising you on movement fore and aft. If anything, it is better to be slightly down by the stern than the bow. If the boat is trimmed properly, it will carry a little *weather helm*. This means that to keep it on its

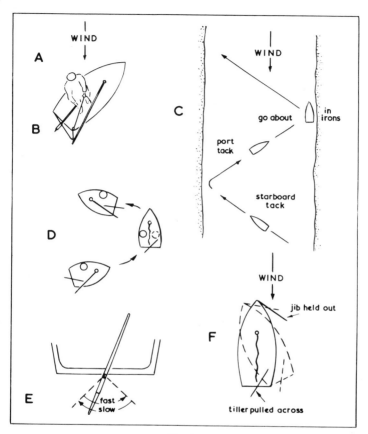

Fig. 12

course you have to pull the tiller slightly towards you (Fig. 12B). In a properly designed boat this is a safety precaution. If there is an accident or you let go of the

45

tiller, the boat will turn into the wind and stop. If there is *lee helm* and you have to keep the tiller pushed away from you on a windward course, when it is let go, the boat turns away from the wind and would run away out of control.

The only way to stop a sailing boat is to turn it into wind. The boat is *in irons*. With the bow pointing upwind, the sails are empty and flap like flags. If you start sailing by getting on a close-hauled course, you can always stop by turning further into the wind.

To get to a point to windward you have to *tack*. You make a zig-zag progress, with each *board* as close to the wind as you can get. When the wind is coming from your port side, you are on the *port tack*, and the other way on the *starboard tack* (Fig. 12C). At the end of each tack you *go about*.

To go about single-handed, make sure there is some way on the boat. If necessary, turn slightly off the wind so as to gain speed, then use your tiller to turn the boat into the wind. Do not slam it over hard. Move it at a moderate speed to about 45 degrees. Going much past this point merely acts as a brake. The sail will come in of its own accord. Keep the rudder over and continue past the point of head into wind. While this is happening (Fig. 12D), you change sides so as to be on the new windward side when the sail begins to fill on the other tack. You also change hands. Be ready to get up to windward if the wind is strong enough to warrant it, but do not climb on to the gunwale or side deck and tilt the boat the wrong way. You regulate your weight to balance the wind pressure in the sail.

Having gone about, you sail until you need to go about again. At first you will fail to go about and *miss stays*. A dodge which may get you past the *eye of the wind* (with bow into wind) is to scull around with the rudder. Jerk the tiller hard in the direction you want the stern to go, then return it slowly to have another go. This is a method frowned on as lubberly by the expert, but if you are stuck, it gets you there (Fig. 12E).

A snag with EPS boats is their extreme lightness. This means that they do not *carry their way*. When you approach the point of going about you need to be moving at as good a speed as possible, otherwise as you turn into the wind and you lose the drive of your sails, the boat will stop, where a heavier boat would keep going by its own momentum. Consequently sculling around with the rudder may have to be the accepted thing in light airs.

If the boat has a jib, its correct handling also helps to make the boat go about. When normally sailing, the angle of the jib should be about the same as the main sail. With two in the boat, the helmsman handles the tiller and the main sheet, which he keeps in his hand. It is never advisable to make the main sheet fast in a small boat. In emergency, you let go the sheet, or allow it to slide through your hands and spill air. If you have a mate, he handles the jib sheets — one each side, although he only uses the one on the lee side. He also deals with the centreboard, but while you are learning, this remains down.

Sailing close-hauled with a jib, you come up to the point where you intend going about. Avoid *pinching* by trying to sail too close to the wind. The aft edge of the sail fluttering is a sign that you are doing this. Maintain your speed and tell your crew your intention by saying 'Ready about' or 'Lee ho'. He does nothing yet with his sail, but you turn the boat with the rudder and change sides and hands, as with the single sail rig. The jib stays to the original side until the crew sees the mainsail fill, then he moves the jib over. All this time, you and your crew are watching the trim of the boat and adjusting your weight accordingly.

Suppose you get into irons. It is possible to push the bow round by *backing the jib*. If your crew hauls or holds out the jib on the wrong side (Fig. 12F), the wind will strike it on the back and push the bow round. Like sculling with the rudder, the expert may regard backing the jib as a sign of lubberliness, but it gets you out of difficulty and even the experts do it on occasions.

It is worthwhile sailing close-hauled as much as possible while learning, as this gives you the feel of the wind and you cannot come to harm. Follow by easing the sheet and *reaching* across the wind. Hold your course with the tiller and adjust your sheet so that you keep course with little load on the tiller. If you haul in the sheet too much the boat will try to turn into the wind. You may also heel excitingly. By all means do this if you want fun, but if you want the boat to sail at its maximum speed, adjust your weight to keep it near upright. This applies to normal hulls. For some of the unusual shapes there are some special considerations which are discussed later in the chapter.

At the end of a reach it should be quite easy to turn into wind and go about in the same way as when sailing close-hauled (Fig. 13A). Reaching backwards and forwards on an open stretch of water can be a pleasant relaxation and a useful instruction time for the children.

Most beginners expect that sailing downwind will be easiest. It is certainly easy to go the way the wind drives you, but you have less control and cannot stop without sufficient space to turn into the wind, and that takes time even if you have space. In light airs you can get away with anything, but in a bit of a blow you could find yourself in difficulties downwind. Consequently, it is better to go little further off the wind than reaching while feeling your way at sailing.

The problem when running is *gybing* (pronounced 'jibing'). This is when the sail changes from one side to the other, as it does when going about, but this time it has the wind in it and may slam over hard. If a gybe is unexpected, the boom could hit someone on the head, some damage could be done to the rigging, or there might even be a capsize. Sometimes a gybe is intentional particularly in light airs, and that is a different matter. Because of the risk of a gybe when running, it is better to sail with the wind slightly to one side of astern than to have it directly astern if conditions allow (Fig. 13B). There is then less risk of the wind catching the back of the sail and bringing it over.

To change from a reach to a *run*, pay out the main

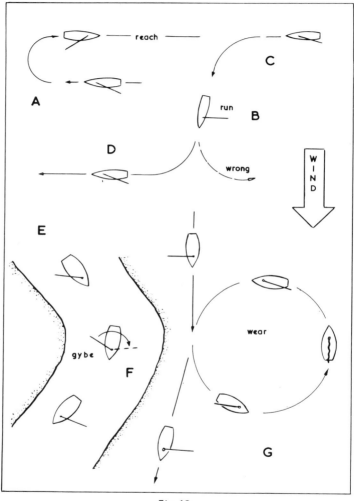

Fig. 13

sheet and use the tiller to turn the boat off the wind (Fig. 13C). When you are moving with the wind, things suddenly become peaceful and the beginner may think that the wind has dropped. This is because the wind is no longer blowing at you as you progress against or across it. Look at marks ashore and you may be surprised how fast you are moving with the wind. Be careful how you turn when you decide to come off the run. If there is room, turn towards the side away from the mainsail (Fig. 13D). As you come round, haul in the main sheet, but not too quickly. Once the boat is across the wind you can haul in and let the sail drive, but before that, too hasty hauling of the sheet may still let the wind get the wrong side and cause a gybe.

Suppose you are going downwind on a river and a bend in the river necessitates turning the boat towards the side the main sail is on (Fig. 13E). If the wind is fairly light and you think a gybe will not be dangerous, warn your crew to keep low and be prepared to move to trim the boat when the sail comes over. Use the rudder to move the boat towards its new course. Gather in the main sheet a little and the wind will almost certainly immediately catch the sail aback and it will gybe (Fig. 13F). If you are prepared for it, a gybe is a perfectly acceptable manouevre.

If you think a gybe might be risky and there is room to turn the boat in a complete circle, it is possible to wear the boat around. In oldtime sailing 'wear' was also applied to going about into wind, but this use is more common today. The advantage is that the main sail

51

changes sides when empty of wind. Turn to the side away from that on which the main sail is. Haul in the sheet a little. Continue around until the bow is into the wind. If your light EPS boat has lost way by then, the jib can be backed to continue around until you are on a reach and can pay off the wind until you are on the new course (Fig. 13G).

When running, weight in the boat can be farther aft than when on other courses. The pressure on the sail is trying to bury the bow, so weight towards the stern keeps the bow up. It is also a help in getting maximum speed if the centreboard or other retractable keel is raised, either all the way or part way up. This reduces the drag, although some boats may yaw if the keel is raised completely. The jib is not so much use when running. It tends to get blanketed by the main sail and may flap ineffectually behind it. This does not matter, as its area is not usually enough to make much difference to speed. One way of using it is to *goosewing* it. It is pulled out to the opposite side to the main sail, either with the sheet, maybe holding by hand, or by a stick (Fig. 14A).

Of course, sailing is not always a simple matter of applying the basic manouevres. When sailing on a river, the wind may be coming diagonally. This means that one way the boat can follow the course of the river on something between a reach and a run, called a *broad reach*. The other way is tacking, but as the wind and river course do not coincide, a course the same angle to the wind each way works out as a sort of saw-tooth progress in relation to the river banks, doing little more

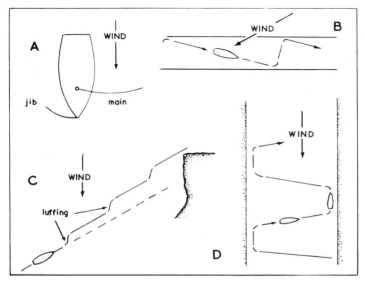

Fig. 14

than cross the river on one leg while making a worthwhile gain on the other (Fig. 14B).

It is sometimes possible to gain a little more to windward, possibly to clear an obstruction without having to go about again, by sailing *full and bye*. Sail towards the obstruction as close hauled as you reasonably can while maintaining way on the boat, then *luff up* into the wind, letting the boat carry its way to the point where you judge it is necessary to pay off and fill the sails again (Fig. 14C). Repeat this operation several times as you approach the object and you may just sail past.

If you want to sail into the wind on a rather narrow river, you may be able to do little more than sail across the river, without making any progress on each board, because of the need to fill the sails and get the boat moving before getting closer to the wind and by then you are across the river. If your boat will carry its way, even a small amount, it is possible to sail across with all the speed you can get, then turn into the wind and let the boat make what progress it can while in irons, before going about completely (Fig. 14D).

It will be seen from all that has been said so far, the safe position to be in is head to wind. Remember this when getting under way or coming into a buoy, a beach or a landing stage.

In some instances it is better to get the boat out into clear water and lie to an anchor or a buoy while hoisting sail. The boat will then naturally weathercock and should stay head to wind unless there is a contrary current also affecting the boat, but so long as the sheets are loose, the sails flap like flags and are harmless, until you prepare to sail away.

Some small boats cannot conveniently be rigged afloat. Those with sleaved sails have to be fitted to their spars before these are fixed in the boat. Even with some other rigs, it is a help to be able to get the adjustment you want while on dry land. In many circumstances it is possible to get away from the shore fully rigged.

If the wind is blowing along the shore, the boat can be rigged ashore or put in the water with the bow into wind and rigged there. If someone gives the bow a push

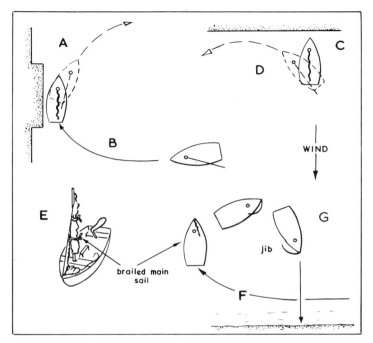

Fig. 15

off, you are away, sailing close-hauled or turning on to a reach (Fig. 15A). To return to this stage, sail towards it, slightly downwind, then luff up as you approach, trying to judge the curved course the boat will take to finish alongside (Fig. 15B). If you fail first time, this is not a difficult situation in which to sail off and try again.

If the wind is blowing offshore, sailing is almost as easy. If the boat is already rigged, it is launched stern first and kept that way. If you are on a beach, the helmsman can clamber in while the crew wades and holds the bow to wind (Fig. 15C). When all is ready he pushes the bow around a little and climbs in ready to lower the centreboard as soon as there is sufficient depth (Fig. 15D). If it is a landing stage, things are much the same except that no-one need get wet. Returning under these conditions is a case of sailing straight for the shore and raising the centreboard at the last moment. Once the centreboard is up, the boat is liable to turn broadside. It may be advisable to lower the jib and sail the last stretch with the main sail only.

If the wind is blowing onshore, either completely or at an angle, it may not be possible to sail off. The boat may have to be rowed or paddled off and the sail hoisted with the boat head to wind at anchor or a buoy. An alternative is to rig the boat completely ashore, then lower the jib ready for hoisting again and haul the main sail into the mast with short *brails*. These are ropes tied with bows or slip knots and they hold the sail in a bundle (Fig. 15E). When the boat has been got far enough offshore, the main sail is broken out by slipping the knots of the brails and you sail away before the wind has driven you back on the shore.

Coming in to a beach in an onshore wind may need a similar technique, unless you find a smooth patch of seaweed and drive straight on! That would be the only way to stop the boat if you sail in. The alternative is to sail in on a reach if possible, rather than a run (Fig. 15F). Do not come so close that you have to raise the centreboard, and allow for the drift when reaching. Turn up into the wind, brail up the main sail if it cannot be lowered easily, and let the jib run you ashore (Fig. 15G).

Some time in your sailing experience you will capsize. In the average boat, which is modestly rigged for family sailing rather than racing, an accidental capsize is rare, but you should know what to do and it is a good idea to pick a nice warm day when you are suitably dressed and go through the drill on a calm stretch of water.

Remember that your EPS boat is very buoyant and will keep you afloat and still have very little difference in draft if full of water. Unlike most heavier boats, if yours is a boat with a centreboard case, when it is righted, the buoyancy is such that the boat floats high enough for any water above the case to run out through the slot. With heavier boats, if the righted boat has water above the case it will float deep and have to be bailed with a bucket while you are still in the water before you can climb in.,

If you capsize, the boat will go over away from the wind and float on its side with the mast and sail flat on the water. There is a considerable amount of boat above the water. If there is much wind, it will not only drive the boat along, it may turn it right over. Your object must be to prevent this. If the boat is completely inverted you may need the help of another boat to right it.

If there is a centreboard or other keel, lever on this to pull the boat up (Fig. 16A). Whether you stand on it

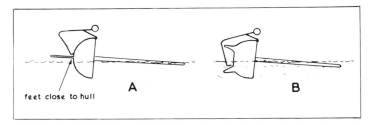

Fig. 16

close in to the hull or pull on it depends on the type of boat. With twin keel craft you may have to get your body around the hull so that you can push one keel with your feet while pulling on the gunwales with your hands (Fig. 16B). Once the boat is up, prevent it going over the other way. If there are two of you, get to opposite sides, but it will be a help if the crew is towards the bow. His drag in the water acts as a sort of mooring buoy and the boat should swing head to wind. If you have a bucket or bailer, that can be used while you are still in the water. When the water inside is down to a reasonable level, climb in. With most boats in EPS it is probably wisest to climb over the transom while your mate, if you have one, holds at the bow. You then get rid of all the water you can and trim the boat while your mate climbs in.

Sometimes it is advisable to lower either partly or completely, one or both sails, or make them ineffective, by slackening a sprit or boom. Any action that will put the sail out of shape, reduces its drawing power and makes it less likely to try to turn the boat over again or sail it away from you.

All that has been said about sailing so far in placid waters is also applicable to sea sailing, but waves make sailing that much more exciting. An EPS boat is more on the surface than boats of other materials. This means that your boat is fairly lively and you must be prepared for the boat tossing and rolling. Choose your occasion and do not make early trips in strong winds.

When the top of a wave is breaking, you can expect spray or more solid water to come on board. If the waves are not breaking, you are likely to ride over most of them. It may be something of a switchback ride, but it should be a comparatively dry one. A heavier boat would be turned into each wave, but with an EPS boat you can keep going. Ease the main sheet a little at each wave, but the jib may be kept sheeted in if you are close-hauled.

Launching or recovering in surf on a pebble beach can cause surface damage to any boat. With polystyrene, this is where you collect dents and scratches. It is unlikely that damage will be serious. It is possible that where damage to a hard-skinned boat might be serious, the EPS merely gets a sizeable dent. However, you want to preserve the appearance of your hull, so take precautions.

When working through surf you must be prepared to get wet, so when launching, it is advisable to manhandle the boat through the breaking surf while wading and to get over the side before the boat touches when returning. As these boats are so light it is possible to take some of the weight rather than let the waves pound the hull on stones. Going afloat, the shallow draught allows you to get the boat wholly supported by water before climbing in. Coming ashore it should not be difficult to get the boat far enough up the beach to be wholly supported by solid ground almost in one movement.

If you are working off a beach used by other people, be careful of bathers. The material of the hull is more of a cushion than other boat materials, but even then it could give a serious blow to a child in the surf.

A boat *broaches to* if it gets out of control and is sideways on to the waves. In the very buoyant EPS boats this is not serious as you will continue to ride over the waves, unless you are close inshore and the waves are breaking, when you will probably be rolled over in the shallow water. The thing to do is get sailing again, rather than lie making no progress with the waves coming at the stationary boat from the side.

Many racing dinghies will *plane*, lifting partly out of the water so that they are supported on the rear half of the bottom. An EPS hull is already well out of the water and it may be possible to get one on to a plane in a good breeze. The boat must be upright and a slight chop on the water is an aid to getting 'unstuck'. Weight should be a little more aft than usual. As the boat rises, the load on the tiller will be felt to increase and it must be held steady. Maybe this is not very likely with your boat, but it is an experience you may have when you have acquired some skill at sailing.

With a powerful outboard motor the sea sled hull of the Scoobee-Doo is capable of high speeds, and will tow a water skier.

Gemini carries a useful area of sail in its gunter sloop rig.

Gemini has a roomy interior. Mast shroud fitting are inside the hull. Thwarts and side benches have plywood tops.

The stern of Gemini has a wooden reinforcement to take an outboard motor.

You will have to get to know your own boat and will soon learn ways to make it sail better. With some hulls, particularly those of special underwater form, with twin keels or bottoms which have that effect, it may be better to give the boat a slight list to leeward to get a greater depth of keel surface when reaching or tacking. How much is something to learn by experience. This is contrary to the usual rule that a boat sails best when level. Trim when running may also have to be adjusted to suit the boat. Instead of a level hull with weight aft, one EPS boat seems to behave better with a list away from the side and sail is.

Most of the EPS boats have rigs which make no provision for *reefing* . In more ambitious craft the area of sail can be reduced in strong winds, making for safety and more efficiency — nothing is to be gained by over-canvassing a boat. A sleeved sail cannot be reefed unless there is an extra sleeve to take the boom and provision for gathering up the surplus below. If the sail is not sleeved on the mast, it may be possible to roll the bottom of the sail around the boom and re-attach that to the mast. As the normal sail areas of EPS small craft are fairly modest, it is unlikely that they will be used in conditions where reefing would be advisable. If you are sailing and the wind increases, it can be spilled by easing the sheets. There is a tendency for a beginner to want to hang on tight to everything, but in emergency always let the sheets slide through your hands. This takes the pressure off the boat and gives you time to think. It is your only speed control. Experiment by reaching in a steady breeze. It is possible to ease the sheets until the sails are barely drawing and the boat is only just moving. Hauling in increases the speed until you get to the correct sail setting for the attitude of the boat. Hauling in further will try to turn the boat into the wind, which has to be corrected by the rudder, and this slows the boat.

Chapter 5

WATERMANSHIP

IF this is your first boat you may wonder where you can use it. Fortunately, in Britain no-one can live more than a couple of hours car journey from the sea and an Ordnance Survey Map of any part of the country shows a plentiful pattern of blue lines. Not every piece of water is available for boating, but an enormous amount is. As far as practical considerations are concerned, EPS craft are so buoyant that many will float in a few inches of water and waterways unsuitable for most other craft have possibilities.

The legal position in Britain is rather confused. There is a right to use tidal waters without fee or the need to ask permission, except for a few particular cases. This means that you can use you boat almost all around the coast without hindrance. Use of the water does not include free access to it. There are many places where you can get on to tidal water over public ground, but elsewhere you may have to ask permission and pay a fee to launch. In harbours you should consult the harbourmaster and may have to pay harbour dues. At many popular resorts there are speed restrictions imposed up to a certain distance offshore, for the common good, and in many places there are areas specified for fast boats and water ski-ing. Usually you can go up tidal inlets or the estuaries of rivers as far as the tide goes without resitrction or fee.

The Norfolk Broads are almost entirely tidal, but there you must have a licence issued by the Great Yarmouth Port & Haven Commissioners, 21 South Quay, Great Yarmouth. It is possible to get this licence on arrival from shops at many of the popular centres.

On non-tidal waters the law says that the bed of the river or lake belongs to whoever owns the banks, with opposite landowners owning up to halfway. The public have no more nor less right to go over this land with water on it than they have over the dry land. As with dry land, a great number of public rights of way have been established on waterways. Many of the larger rivers, which have been used for navigation for hundreds of years are rights of way, either for their whole length or for part of it. The Severn is a right of way from the source to where it becomes tidal near Gloucester. Most of the Trent, most of the Wye, the Avon from Stratford down and many other rivers are rights of way. There are not so many lakes where there are rights, but Windermere and Ullswater, in the Lake District and Loch Lomond, in Scotland are available.

The popular non-tidal Thames above Teddington Lock is a special case as it is controlled by the Thames Conservancy, Burdett House, 15 Buckingham Street, London WC2. A licence must be obtained from them before putting a boat on the river. Their staff cannot issue licences on the spot.

A Thames Conservancy licence now includes use of the locks, all of which are staffed and worked for you. Elsewhere on some of the rivers which are rights of way, there are locks and a fee is charged for their use, although use of the river is free.

There is a network of canals linking rivers and it is possible to use them to make long journeys without removing your boat from the water. Some of the canals are no longer in a fit state for commercial traffic, but they can still be used for pleasure boating. An EPS boat is particularly suitable for some where locks do not work or swing bridges no longer swing, as it can be lifted out and carried round with little effort.

Canals were dug as commercial ventures. Although few of them ever showed a profit, they must still be regarded as businesses and a payment made for use of them. Most canals are controlled by the British Waterways Board, Pleasure Craft Licencing Office, Willow Grange, Church Road, Watford, Herts. A licence should be obtained in advance.

Most canals have plenty of locks and a journey on a canal is best reckoned in locks rather than miles, as they control the amount of progress and too many locks in a day make for hard work. However, a lock is interesting to operate and many people find fascination in a canal cruise, as some of them pass through beautiful scenery (The Llangollen Canal is a good example) and they need a special attitude of mind — you take pleasure from pleasant surroundings and leisurely progress. Do not regard your local dirty canal by the gasworks as typical.

A good guide to places to launch boats on tidal and non-tidal waters in the British Isles in the annual *Getting Afloat* (Link House, Dingwall Avenue, Croydon, Surrey, CR9 2TA.). This contains details of well over one thousand ramps and similar places. A good guide to boating facilities around the coast, as well as a mine of information on a great many boating matters, is the annual *Boat World* (Business Dictionaries Ltd., Sell's House, 39 East Street, Epsom, Surrey). A good general map of inland waters is *Stanford's Inland Cruising Map of England* (Edward Stanford Ltd., 12-14 Long Acre, London WC2.). The same publisher also offers charts of several coastal areas. The British Waterways Board issues guide books to several of the popular canals.

If you are taking your boat abroad, the legal position in most nearby continental countries is easier, with freedom to use waters more general, often including free use of locks.

Locks

OPERATING a lock is not difficult if tackled logically. Most locks have a pair of gates at each end arranged in a V pointing towards the higher level (Fig. 17A) so that water pressure keeps them closed. In the gates are sliding doors to let water through (Fig. 17B). In some cases the doors slide over channels in the lock sides, but the effect is the same. The doors are called 'paddles' and they are operated through a rack and pinion arrangement by a crank handle, called a 'windlass'. On

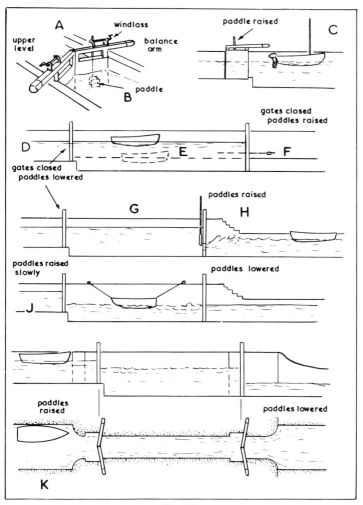

Fig. 17

most waterways you hire or buy your own windlass.

The lock is a sort of water lift. You fill or empty it to raise or lower your boat. Obviously the paddles at both ends should not be open at the same time, or you will merely allow water to run right through. Suppose you arrive at the top of a lock and find the level the same inside as you are on. The paddles will be raised and you can push the gates open and take the boat in (Fig. 17C). Most gates have an extending balance arm. You get your back against it and heave the gate open. When the boat is in, you close the gates and lower the paddles (Fig. 17D). Go to the lower gates and raise their paddles, so that the level inside the lock begins to fall (Fig. 17E). Be patient until the level in the lock matches that on the lower pound, then push the gates open and the boat moves out (Fig. 17F).

If you arrive at the bottom and find the water level down inside, the procedure is much the same in reverse, except that when filling a lock, do not open the top paddles too wide at first, otherwise the water surges in, the wave hits the lower gate and rebounds, so that the boat surges about. Even with lines to the bollards or rings provided, it is difficult to control the boat. Start with only a little opening. When the lock is half full, open up more and gradually raise the paddles completely.

If you arrive at a lock which is 'against you' and has water in it at the opposite level to what you want, your work is doubled. Suppose you arrive at the lower level and find the lock full (Fig. 17G). Moor a little distance below the lock, see that the top gates and paddles are closed, then open the bottom paddles (Fig. 17H). There is quite a flurry of water below the lock as the paddles are open — hence the advisability of mooring out of this area. When the lock is empty, the boat is taken in, the bottom gates and paddles closed, then filling commences (Fig. 17J). When you arrive at the top and find the lock empty, there is no need to moor far away as the water above is not disturbed as you fill the lock (Fig. 17K). Finding the locks for or against you can make a lit of difference to your work and progress on a much-locked canal, so it is sometimes worthwhile waiting until a boat passes you the opposite way, then locks ahead will be found in your favour.

Tides

AROUND the British coast the duration of each tide is rather more than 12 hours. If high water at one place is at noon today, it will occur again at about 20 minutes after midnight and about 20 minutes to 1 pm next day. After a fortnight the time of high water will be about noon again. The time of low water varies, but the duration of ebb tide is usually longer than the flood (rising) tide — perhaps 7 hours ebb and 5 hours flood. During the period of full and new moon there are spring tides, which rise higher and drop lower, and consequently run faster. Midway between are neap tides, with the least rise and fall.

Tidal streams approach the British Isles from the Atlantic, hitting the corner of the mainland at Cornwall and dividing to go up the Irish Sea and Bristol Channel or along the English Channel. The stream up the west coast goes around the north of Scotland and down the North Sea to meet the other stream in the vicinity of Dover. This is a simplification, but it gives an idea of the relative tide times.

The amount of rise and fall varies considerably between places. Along the South Coast the difference between high and low water may only be a few feet. In the Bristol Channel it can be 40ft. This means that boating off the shore may be possible for perhaps 6 hours on a tide along the English Channel, but in Bristol Channel places there may only be an hour or so at the top of the tide.

Advance information on tide times can be obtained from local newspapers. In many places there are pocket tide tables available. The basic tidal predictions are given for Dover or London Bridge. Many annual publications give these and a set of constants to add or subtract to get the tide times at other places. Tidal predictions for all British ports are given in nautical almanacs, which are published annually. They contain an enormous amount of other information needed for navigating around the coast, and some are really intended for shipping rather than yachting. For yachtsmen the most useful almanac is *Reed's Nautical Almanac* (Thomas Reed Publications Ltd., 39 St. Andrew's Hill, London EC4.).

Coastal boating

THE owner of an EPS boat launching into tidal waters for a few hours family boating in a bay or harbour need not get involved in very advanced navigation or pilotage,

fisherman. Beside tide times you need to know how fast the tidal streams may be (half ebb is usually fastest), any rocks or sandbanks which may be exposed and any other hazards or limits. Consider wind direction in relation to the coast, and the tide. While there may be good safe sailing at high water, if wind and flood tide are in the same direction, you may not be able to sail back again an hour or so after the ebb starts. When the tide changes, wind against tide may cause quite lively waves, perhaps rougher than you were expecting. Think ahead in relation to your return. What will the conditions be in a few hours time? If you are letting the children go afloat alone, can they cope with an adverse tide or are they strong enough to row back if necessary?

Do not be frightened of using your boat on the sea, but tidal waters should not be treated casually. You may come to no harm as a result of ignorance on most inland waters, but at sea you may get into difficulty if not danger, if you have not prepared in a seamanlike way.

If you want to go somewhere, rather than potter locally off a beach, you should learn the elements of pilotage (finding your way from point to point along the coast) if not with navigation (which is concerned with going out of sight of land). Many general boating books give you this information. You need a compass suitable for taking bearings and a chart.

but it is a wise precaution to take local advice, although not every man in a peaked cap and a blue jersey leaning over the rail is an expert. Ask the harbour-master or a

Admiralty charts give a terrific amount of information, but they are intended for large craft, except for a few yachtsmen's charts of popular yachting centres. For the small boat man Edward Stanford (12-14 Long Acre, London WC2.) publish coloured charts with many courses laid off and other work done for you. For the areas these cover, they are probably your best guide. More yachtsmen's charts covering these and other areas are published by Imray and Wilson (Wych House, St. Ives, Hunts.).

If you plan to make a coastal trip, it is advisable to let someone know of your intentions and your estimated times at various places. It is unlikely that anything will go wrong, but if it does, searchers have something to work on. When you have completed the trip, let the same person know that it is over. For an ambitious coastal trip you should tell the coastguards, again with as much detail as possible. They will observe you and you will be passed from one to another. When you have finished, or if you alter your plans, let them know.

Weather when you are boating is much more than 'Shall I take a mac?'. Wind, fog, rain as well as sun, affect boating conditions, even to the point of being hazards rather than just discomfort or pleasure. Get forecasts before you venture offshore. The ordinary general radio forecasts are of value, but there are better ones. The shipping forecasts and reports from coastal weather stations have your needs in mind. They are given in an abbreviated form which follows a standard pattern. A full explanation is given in the book *Weather*

Forecasts (Royal Yachting Association, 5 Buckingham Gate, London SW1.). It is possible to get forecasts by telephone from meteorological offices or reports of actual weather from the coastal weather stations. These are free. A full list is given in the book mentioned.

Incidentally, the above book is only one of a large series available free to members of the RYA, or at a fee to others. If you become an individual member, you will be helping the organisation which looks after your interests and can recover the fee paid in the value of useful books obtained.

Buoys

WHEN you boat in an estuary or tidal inlet you will find buoys and other guides for craft using the waters. In general these mark channels suitable for larger craft than yours. You may be able to float elsewhere with your slight draughts, but as the tide drops you may be glad to know what the buoys mean if you are not to be left for six hours or so isolated on a sandbank

The shape of a buoy indicates which side of the channel it is. If it is can-shaped (Fig. 18A) it is to be passed on your port hand (left side) when entering with the flood stream. If it is conical (Fig. 18B) it should be passed on your starboard hand when entering on the flood tide. When leaving on the ebb tide, obviously the buoys will be on the opposite side of the boat. Port hand buoys may be red all over or red and white chequer. Starboard hand buoys may be black all over or black and white chequer.

If there is a sandbank or other obstruction at the

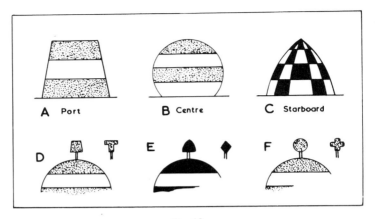

Fig. 18

centre of a channel, it is marked with spherical buoys at the inner and outer ends (Fig. 18C). If the main channel is to the right, on the flood tide, there are red and white horizontal bands and a red can top mark at the outer end and a T shape at the inner end (Fig. 18D). If the main channel is to the left, there are black and white horizontal bands and a conical top mark at the outer end and a diamond at the inner end (Fig. 18E). If both channels are of equal important there are red and white horizontal bands, with a ball top mark at the outer end and a cross at the inner end (Fig. 18F).

These are the main navigational buoys. In minor channels, local users sometimes have their own markings, but the colouring often follows buoyage practice. There may be perches (posts in the mud), painted red and white bands or an all-over black to mean the same as these colours on buoyss.

Although there are many other buoys, others are less common and can be learned as you progress in pilotage knowledge. Green is reserved for danger, so any green buoy should be avoided as it marks a wreck. Details of buoys are given on charts, so their identification provides a guide to your location when cruising. On inland waters authorities use marks and buoys to indicate obstructions or shallows, which usually have a family likeness to the buoys used on tidal waters, so their meaning is obvious.

Chapter 6

YOUR BOAT ASHORE

EXPANDED polystyrene is a material soft enough to take surface marks from even thumbnail pressure, but which is unlikely to sustain damage sufficient to be of vital importance. Protective coatings do something to reduce the external marking, but when handling the boat, its particular surface characteristics should be kept in mind if the quality of the surface and the appearance of the boat is to be maintained.

The boat should be carried whenever possible, rather than dragged or even wheeled on a trolley. The extremely light weight of EPS makes carrying feasible with most boats, often by only two people. It is possible for one man to invert many types of boats and walk with a boat supported by a thwart across his shoulders, looking rather like a snail.

If possible put the boat down on a smooth surface. Sand is unlikely to mark the surface and pebbles of even size do not matter much, but the sort of surface to avoid is a gravel path or anywhere else with angular stones. Make it a rule that no-one is allowed to climb in the boat when it is ashore. This is unnecessary, and

The two-part mould for Gemini hulls at the premises of Profile Expanded Plastics.

Another view of the same mould. Polystyrene enters through the tubes. The plate at one side passes through the mould to make a keel slot.

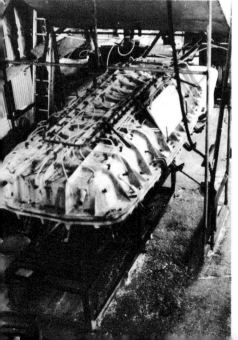

Above Sea Snark has an unstayed mast and a lateen sail.

Below Sea Snark has a mast thwart, but seating is in the bottom of the boat.

apart from any marking inside, the pressure may cause stones underneath to be forced into the skin.

Your boat is unlikely to be damaged when fully afloat or high and dry in a static position. It is hauling in and out and moving ashore that need caution. Beware of willing helpers who have no clue to what they are doing. Even if the boat is apparently static ashore, consider the effect of wind on the light hull. It could be lifted and moved bodily by a moderate breeze. If the boat is left unattended in the open, one or more webbing straps across it to pegs in the ground would be a sensible precaution.

As the material can be dented by local pressure, it is as well to spread any load under holding-down arrangement, so webbing is better than rope.

Most EPS boats are light enough for two to lift on to a car roof and in most circumstances this is the best way to transport them. However, apart from the weight, windage is a consideration and a large deep hull could cause problems in high cross-winds. The alternative is a trailer, but this brings legal problems, apart from the mechanical ones concerned with towing attachments. The pattern of car lights and number plate have to be reproduced on the trailer, usually on a board cramped to the boat. The speed limit, outside normal limit areas, is the same as when towing a caravan.

When loading a boat, either on a trailer or a roof rack, it is important to spread the area of contact as much as possible at the points of support. The commonest roof racks for boats consist of two crossbars with no

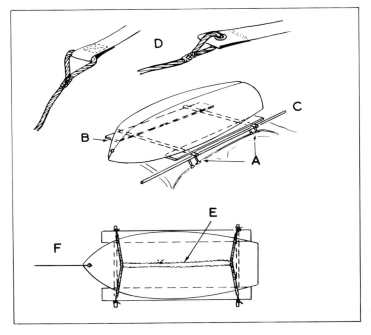

Fig. 19

connection between them, supported either on pads or directly on the car roof gutters (Fig. 19A). The boat rides steadiest if these are located as far apart as possible. If an EPS boat is lashed on these racks without anything to spread the load, the crossbars will press grooves in the hull.

How the load is spread depends on the particular boat, but for one which travels inverted, two light planks lashed or bolted on will cover a good length of each gunwale (Fig. 19B). For a boat to be carried the right way up there could be shaped and padded supports mounted on the racks. However, although some makers advocate carrying the right way up, many experienced small boat men would rather have the boat upside-down. The car and boat make a more streamlined combination. With the boat the right way up, it is possible to carry things inside, but rain can add an unwanted and unstable ballast, which may affect control of the car. If the boat is inverted, all loose gear has to be removed and carried elsewhere, but this is preferable if it gives safe driving. Spars can usually be lashed under or on the side of the racks (Fig. 19C).

Some builders of EPS boats offer racks to suit and provide plastic or other supports to spread the loads at support points. Obviously, these should be considered when buying the boat, if an existing rack is not there to be adapted. Usually, an inverted hull can be lifted on by two people from the side, keeping rubbing and sliding to as little as possible.

Ropes for holding down may mark the hull. Webbing about 2in. wide, such as is sold for toe streaps in racing dinghies, is better, but the ends should have rope tails for tying down (Fig. 19D). The ends can be turned back and sewn, then the rope taken through the loop formed or through an eyelet. The knot to use to secure to a firm point on the rack is the round turn and two half hitches (Fig. 5D). Because of the curve of the inverted hull, with many boats it is advisable to put a rope between the holding down straps (Fig. 19E) to prevent them slipping down over the tapered ends. If the boat has a painter attachment outside the bow, a rope can be taken forward to the car bumper (Fig. 19F). Main attachments are to the rack. Anything else should be regarded as supplementary.

It is not impossible to carry an EPS boat inverted without a rack, although this should only be regarded as a temporary measure. A blanket, or other padding, goes on the car roof and the boat goes directly on that.

Most boat owners get a lot of satisfaction out of doing things to their boat. The basic boat is likely to have all essential gear, but it will not be long before most owners think of additions or alterations they would like to make. It is possible to get too gadget-conscious, but some extras will personalize your boat.

There are cleats, fairleads, blocks and other fittings, which may be better than those originally supplied. There may be different ropes you favour or you may think of a different way of having the rigging arranged. Within the boat you may want to add lockers or stowage space. It is possible to attach to EPS with epoxy resin glue, but it may be better to build a locker under a thwart (Fig. 20A) or attach to some other existing wooden part. Rowlocks can be stowed through holes in the main thwart (Fig. 20B). They can be provided with lanyards to prevent loss overboard (Fig. 4A).

A bailer or a plastic bucket will be needed to get unwanted water out of the boat. This should have a

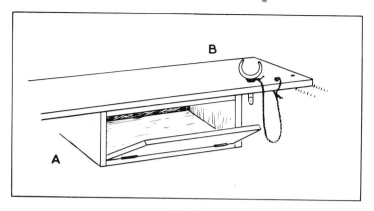

Fig. 20

lanyard to secure it to a thwart or other point — it is after you capsize that you need it most and it is no use if it has washed away. A canvas or stout plastic bag fixed to the side of the centreboard case, or elsewhere, makes a good stowage place for oddments, especially if it has a plastic zip fastener or press studs.

Two or more fenders are worth having, to hang over the side of the boat and prevent damage when coming alongside. A boathook is worth carrying. It need not be more than a few feet long, and choose one with a double-hooked end, rather than one with a spike, which may damage your boat or someone elses.

You ought to name your boat. It may not be a satisfactory job to paint directly on the EPS, but you could put the names with transfer letters on a piece of plywood to mount inside the transom.

Chapter 7

REPAIRS AND MAINTENANCE

EXPANDED polystyrene does not suffer from exposure to the weather. It can be left outside to be heated by the sun or soaked by rain and snow. These things will not affect its durability, but outside storage without protection is likely to make the material dirty to the extent where it cannot be cleaned. There is also the effect of climatic conditions on other materials in the boat. Moisture may get under varnish and stain wood. If conditions drop below freezing, the ice formed in the wood takes up more room than water and may crack the veneers of plywood. Steel parts are liable to rust, even if plated. Brass may crack in freezing conditions.

Obviously, it is better to hang the boat in the roof of a garage or store it in some other way indoors. Polythene sheeting around it will keep it clean. Spread the load if hanging up. Use wide webbing rather than rope, or suspend on broad strips of wood (Fig. 21A). If the boat has to be kept outside, it might be raised and polythene sheeting arranged like a tent (Fig. 21B). This allows air to circulate and avoids condensation, which will not affect the polystyrene, but might damage wood

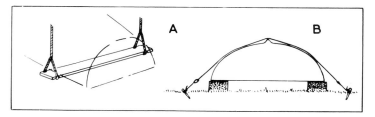

Fig. 21

or metal.

Beside the need to keep polystyrene away from flames or excessive heat, there are several liquids which will dissolve the material. Although the result of contact with one is not a sudden disappearance of the material, the surface will be eaten away and damaged, so accidental contact must be dealt with quickly. Some common solvent liquids are petrol, oil, white spirit, acetone, turpentine (or 'turps. substitute') and carbon tetrachloride (cleaning fluid). Methylated spirits does not affect polystyrene, so this is a useful fluid for removing any of the others. It can also be used for removing the oily and tarry marks around the waterline after the boat has been used in polluted water. Ordinary domestic detergents are safe to use on polystyrene, so dirt may be scrubbed off with them.

Petrol and oil are the things most likely to give trouble. If these come into contact with the unprotected polystyrene, mop them with rags or tissues, which are then discarded away from the boat. If methylated spirit is available, wipe the affected part with plenty of spirit to dilute the petrol or oil and remove with tissues. If spirit is unavailable, water can be used, but this does not mix with petrol or oil and can only be expected to disperse them with the aid of rags or tissues.

When a boat is sold for regular use with an outboard motor the area where this will be is already protected by the makers. There may be a plastic moulding or tray or the surface may be given a petrol-proof coating.

A polystyrene boat with a surface direct from moulding is cheapest and this is how most boats are supplied. With reasonable care this may have a worthwhile life, but even the most carefully-used boat is likely to finish a season looking rather shabby. Most boats are offered with protective coatings, or kits for applying you own, at extra cost. A boat without treatment, which has become shabby, may have its appearance improved by painting. Of course, a new boat may also be painted and the colour touched up as wear takes place.

Because the solvent in many paints will attack polystyrene, the makers' recommendations should be considered. With a new boat there is also the problem of release agent which is left on the surface after moulding. If this is not removed, it affects the adhesion of paint and causes blisters. Use methylated spirit fairly liberally and tissues which are discarded frequently. Working in this way avoids the risk of merely dissolving and spreading the release agent if very little spirit is used.

Follow the detergent and water, but make sure this is

washed off with clean water, as detergent will also affect paints. The surface must be really dry before painting.

If all that is required is colour to smarten a shabby hull or to change the appearance of a new one, a good exterior quality emulsion paint can be used. This is cheap enough and simple enough for coats to be applied as needed during the season.

Marine paint manufacturers are working on the problem of coatings for polystyrene and it is likely that new finishes will come on the market, but otherwise the advice of the boat supplier should be taken. Solvents used in some paints will attach polystyrene. Many paints intended for wood and metal dry to a hard brittle skin. On the soft flexible surface of polystyrene, this would lead to cracking. Most high gloss paints suffer from this trouble. International Paints Ltd., offer a special combination of primer and one-pot polyurethane finish in several bright colours.

Some of the synthetic resins used in paints and that commonly used with glassfibre will attack polystyrene, but solvent-free epoxy resin is safe and satisfactory. Where something more than just a change of colour is needed, epoxy resin finishes offer a good means of protecting the surface. Epoxy resin is resistant to petrol and is very resistant to wear. Colours available are few, but once the surface has been coated, it can be followed with other paints.

Two firms who make epoxy finishes are Unitex Marine, Knaresborough, Yorkshire and Ault & Wiborg Industrial Finishes Ltd., 14/16 Wadsworth Road,

Perivale, Greenford, Middlesex. The finishes recommended for coating polystyrene are solvent-free and are supplied in two parts which have to be mixed together before use. The materials are pastes rather than paints and it is possible to build up any desired thickness. As a guide to quantity, one finish built up to 1/32in. is estimated as covering 54 s.ft. per gallon.

Epoxy resin can be used with glassfibre, so it is possible to coat a boat with resin and bed glass cloth or mat in it, then follow with more resin, in the same way as applying a G.R.P. (glass reinforced plastic) skin to any other boat. Polycell-Prout offer a kit of resin and glassfibre cloth for their Pioneer and other craft.

Isoclad is a plastic finish which is made by Liquid Plastics Ltd., PO Box No. 7, London Road, Preston, Lancs., PR1 4AJ, and which is recommended by most of the makers of polystyrene boats, either alone or with glassfibre. It is a paste which is applied by brush. It dries quickly to form a tough elastic skin with a good bond to the boat. It resists heat and the chemicals which will attack polystyrene. Glassfibre webbing can be pressed into the first coat and followed with a further coat after this is dried. Eleven colours are available, and polyurethane paint can be used over Isoclad. As this is a one-can finish, a small quantity for touching up is more convenient to carry than the two-part epoxy.

Obviously, skinning a boat adds to its weight and some of the attraction of the light weight of polystyrene is lost, but the protection given must be assessed in relation to needs; whether extreme lightness or a tougher skin is to be more important. Skinning adds to first cost. It can be applied later, but if a much-used and pitted boat is to be skinned there will have to be quite a lot of making good of the surface first. It is really much better to decide on skinning, if you think it advisable in your case, before the boat is put into use.

With this new material, calling for a new line of thought, there is also the possibility of regarding the unprotected hull as disposable; taking all the bits and pieces off after a couple of years and buying a new hull to put them on. It could be that as polystyrene boats become more popular and acceptable, costs of the basic moulding as a replacement may offer a favourable alternative to the expense and labout of trying to make the original hull last longer by sheathingg.

Many adhesives have solvents which attack polystyrene. Other adhesives, which may be satisfactory for ceiling tiles and similar things are not suitable for boats. An epoxy resin adhesive is the best choice for attaching wood or other materials to polystyrene. Araldite is the most easily obtainable adhesive or glue of this type.

Standard parts are attached by the makers to wood or metal fittings embedded in the polystyrene. If you want to add something of your own, it is necessary to penetrate the material some way so as to get a good area of cover for the adhesive. Merely gluing to the surface will not withstand more than the smallest strain without the EPS breaking away. Wood dowels are a convenient way of attaching. Drill a slightly undersize hole for a dowel, perhaps 1½in. long and 3/8in. diameter. Smear this and the hole with Araldite and press in. When this has set, the dowel can be drilled to take a fixing screw (Fig. 22A). For a wooden fitting, the dowel can pass through it without the need for a screw (Fig. 22B). Wood strips can be fixed to the bottom or around the gunwale in this way. A rubber or plastic fender moulding around a light wood gunwale strip will protect the part most likely to be disfigured by knocks (Fig. 22C).

For filling dents, one of the fillers sold for use on household plasterwork, such as an external grade of Polyfilla, can be used. This is merely pressed into the hole or dent and left slightly proud of the surface, so that it can be sanded off afterwards. Dent filling in this way should precede repainting or coating.

A hole right through is very unlikely, but possible. As polystyrene is very buoyant, there is no fear of the loss of your boat through sinking, but you want to keep the water out, for comfort, if nothing else. A temporary repair can be made with the self-adhesive waterproof strip sold by canoe firms. This is like Sellotape, but in 2in. or greater width and with a fully-waterproof adhesive. Dry the outside surface, preferably with methylated spirit, and press on the strip. Widths can be made up by overlapping (Fig. 22D). The strip can also be used for protection at points of wear (Fig. 22E).

For a permanent repair, the damage should be squared-up by trimming with a sharp knife, lubricated with soapy water. Give the sides a slight taper from the

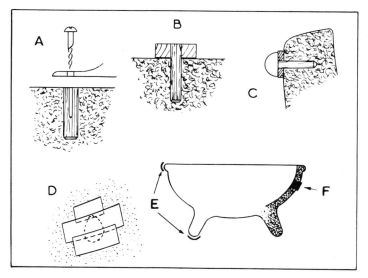

Fig. 22

outside. Cut a block of polystyrene to press into this hole and glue it in place. If necessary, make up the thickness with several pieces. If there is much curve outside, let the repair piece stance above the surface and sand it to shape afterwards (Fig. 22F).

Maintenance and repair of wood parts is straightforward. Do not allow wood to remain bare. It absorbs water and dirt. Polyurethane varnish is more likely to have been used on the original wood parts of your boat. Get a one-can marine-grade polyurethane varnish for touching up. Avoid getting varnish on unprotected EPS. You will probably make a better job of refurbishing a wood part by removing it, in any case.

Sail damage should be attended to quickly. Stitching pulling away or a tiny rip can soon develop into something more serious if you carry on sailing without attending to it. Carry a needle and some terylene thread in your boat kit. It is seamanlike to have a small duffle bag or something similar with a few basic tools, such as screwdriver and pliers, with whatever is needed for an outboard motor and a few emergency repair items. A serviceable clasp knife may be in this bag or on a lanyard around your neck.

SPECIFICATION OF SOME EPS BOATS

Sea Snark

THIS is American in origin, and 60,000 are claimed to have been used there in the nine years it has been in production. In Britain it was handled by the Avon Rubber Co. and latterly by Foley Packaging Co. The hull is a conventional dinghy shape, but rather narrow and shallow for its length — 11ft. (3·35m) long by 38in. (0.96m) beam and 12in. (0·31m) depth — making its form something between a dinghy and a sailing surfboard. A daggerboard trunk is moulded in and the rudder is quite shallow. There is a striped lateen sail on aluminium alloy mast and spars. The mast is supported by a thwart, but the crew (normally two) sit in the bottom of the boat. Total weight is 40lb. (18kg.) (Fig.23A).

Pioneer

THIS is a dinghy of generally-similar proportions and shape to many craft built in other materials. The

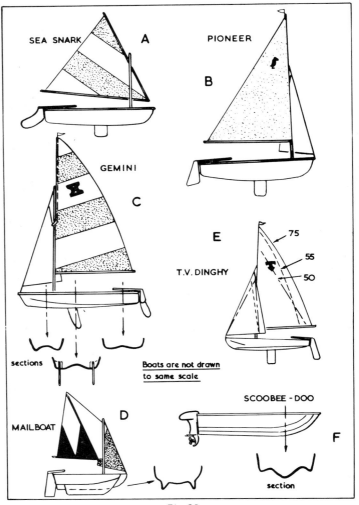

SEA SNARK A

PIONEER B

GEMINI C

E
75
55
50
T.V. DINGHY

sections

Boats are not drawn
to same scale

SCOOBEE - DOO

MAILBOAT D

F

section

Fig. 23

gunwale at the bow is almost semi-circular, but lower down there is a stem effect. A daggerboard case is stiffened by a centre thwart. The mast passes through another thwart and there is seating both at the stern and on side benches and storage compartments. The aft seat converts to a daggerboard.

There is a sleeved Bermudan main sail on an unstayed metal mast. A jib is optional. The hull is 9ft.4in. (2.82m) long and 4ft.6in (1.36m) beam, with a freeboard of 1ft.6in. (0.46m). The main sail area is 41 s.ft. (3.78m²). For use with an outboard motor up to 3½ HP there is a plastic transom cover and tray available. The best sailing crew is two, but more can be carried and under oars or power five is a reasonable number. A skinning kit is available. Makers are Polycell Prout Ltd., Broadwater Road, Welwyn Garden City, Herts. Total weight of the boat, without removable sailing gear, is about 50lb (22.7kg.). The tubular mast is in two sections for ease of transport (Fig. 23B).

Gemini

THIS is a larger boat than the others listed, being 13 ft. (3.96m) long and 5ft. (1.52m) beam, with a hull depth of 1ft.9in. (0.53m). The underwater shape is of sea sled form, with twin bows blending into a conventional single transom. It is made by Stoneham Shaw Ltd., Braintree Road Trading Estate, South Ruislip, Middlesex, and they offer it in several forms, from a hull to complete yourself, through rowing, power and two sailing boats to a power/sailer.

Seating is on a mast thwart, a main thwart, a stern seat and side benches. Lift-out storage bins can be fitted. There are twin hinged keels fairly close to the sides. Normally, only the board on the lee side needs to be lowered, and the boards are changed when going about. The gunter main sail is sleeved on its gaff and is 60 s.ft. (5·57 m²). A 20 s.ft. jib (1·86m²) is optional. The rudder has a hinged blade and the main sail has a kicking strap.

Boats intended for power are sheathed. Quite a small motor will give a reasonable speed, but 15 HP will make the boat plane. The boat alone weighs about 100 lb. (45·4kg.). The makers offer many extras including roof racks and trailers (Fig. 23C).

Mailboat

THIS is a beamy boat for its length — 8ft. (2·44m) by 5ft. (1·52m) — with a 2ft.6in (0·76m) deep hull. For most of its length there are moulded-in bilge keels. There are centre and aft seats and the mast passes through a plywood support at seat level. The main sail is supported by a sprit and a boom. It is 38 s.ft. (3·53m²) and there is a jib of just over 7 s.ft. (0·69m²). The boat may be sailed by one or two and will carry up to four under oars or power. A small long-shaft motor can be used. Weight is 68lb. (30·8kg). Paint and sheathing kits are available.

The suppliers are Daily Mail, Temple House, Temple Avenue, London EC4 (Fig. 23D).

TV Dinghy

SPONSORED by the T.V. Times, this is offered as a rowing boat or with three rigs. The hull form is of fairly conventional dinghy shape, with a stem pointed up to gunwale level and with a chine line showing just above the water forward. Sizes are 11ft.3in. (3·86m) long, 5ft. (1·52m) beam and 21in. (0·53m) deep. There are main and mast thwarts and a daggerboard case forward of the main thwart. There are built-in side benches.

The smallest rig is the TV 50, with a Bermudan sloop rig of 50 s.ft. (4·65m²) on a 14ft.6in.(4·42m) two-part tubular mast. The TV 55 has a more ambitious rig of 55 s.ft. (5.11m²) arranged in the same way. The first is described as a family boat, while the second is also suitable for children racing. For those who want a faster rig there is the TV 75 with 75 s.ft. (6·97m²) on a17ft. (5·18m) sectional mast.

For motors up to 4 HP there is a protection kit available. A special car roof rack for single-handed loading can be bought. Weight is 95 lb. (43kg). The suppliers are T.V. Times Dinghy, 247 Tottenham Court Road, London WIP OAU. (Fig. 23E).

Scoobee-doo

THIS is also by Polycell Prout and is the only boat listed which is intended only for power. There is a plastic-lined engine compartment, which will take the fuel tank of a large motor. While pottering can be with a motor as small as 1½ HP, larger motors will make the boat plane and it is possible to tow a water-skier. For general purposes on the sea, 3 to 5 HP is recommended, while it is claimed that 25 HP will give a speed of 25 mph or tow two skiers. Unprotected hulls are available, but it is recommended that with more than 9 HP the hull should be sheathed.

The hull is 11ft.2in. (3·40m) by 5ft.1in. (1·53m) beam, with a freeboard of about 19in. (0·50m). In plan view the gunwales are almost parallel for the full length, giving a squarish bow over a 'cathedral' hull, with three stems — the centre one being deeper. Extras available include a steering console and a hood. Skinning kits are available. Eyebolts for ski towing are provided. There are wood centre thwart and side benches. With the fixed equipment the boat weighs about 100 lb. (45·4 kg). (Fig. 23F).

Note:— British EPS hulls are moulded by Profile Expanded Plastics Ltd., Kensworth, Bedfordshire.

GLOSSARY

Aback — Wind on the wrong side of the sail
Abeam — A direction at right angles to the centre line of
        the boat
About, to go — To change direction to the opposite tack
Aft — Towards the stern
Amidships — Centre of boat
Araldite — Trade name of an epoxy adhesive
Athwart — Across the boat

Back — Holding a sail so that the wind strikes it on the
        opposite side
Bail, to — Remove water from a boat
Batten — Wood or plastic strip in a pocket in the edge of
        a sail
Beam — The width of a boat
Bear away — Alter direction more to leeward
Beat — Sail to windward close-hauled
Belay — Secure a rope, usually around a cleat
Bermudan sail — A tall triangular main sail
Block — A device containing at least one sheave for
        altering the direction of a rope or providing
        a purchase

Boom — Spar at the foot of a sail

Boom vang — Alternative name for kicking strap

Broach to — To swing broadside to the waves

Broach reach — Sailing with the wind slightly aft of beam

Buoy — Flotaing object anchored to the bottom, indicating a channel or providing a mooring

Burgee — Small flag flown at the masthead as a wind indicator

Centre board (or plate) — Pivoting keel raising into a case

Cleat — Two-pronged fitting for belaying a rope

Clew — Lower aft corner of a sail

Close-hauled — Sailing as close as possible towards the wind

Cut — Common name for canal

Dagger board (or plate) — Keel which lifts up and down in its case or trunk

Dinghy — Small pulling or sailing boat, usually open or partly decked

Draught (or draft) — The depth of water needed to float a boat

Ebb — The stream due to the falling tide

Epoxy — A synthetic resin, used as a glue on EPS

EPS — Expanded polystyrene

Fair — Favourable. A following wind.

Fairlead — Guide for a rope

Fall off — Turn away from the wind when sailing

Fathom — Six feet

Fender — Pad to protect the side of a boat against chafe

Fibreglass — Trade name of one make of glass fibre

Flood — Tidal stream due to a rising tide

Forestay — Mast support to the stem

Forward — Towards the bow

Freeboard — Height of deck or gunwale above the water

Gaff — Spar at the top of a main sail, not passing forward of the mast

Genoa — A large jib sail which overlaps the main sail

Glass fibre — Glass in form of mat or cloth for reinforcing resin

Go about — To change direction to the opposite tack

Gosseneck — Metal universal joint between boom and mast

Goose-winged — Sailing before the wind with the jib on the opposite side to the main sail

G.R.P. — Glass-reinforced resin

Gudgeon — The part of a rudder hanging with a hole

Gunter — A type of main sail in which the gaff continues almost vertically above the mast

Gunwale — Top of the outside of the hull

Gybe — Change direction with the wind aft so that the main sail is blown across the boat

Halyard (Halliard) — Rope for hoisting a sail or flag

Harden in — Tighten

Headboard — Board fixed in the head of a triangular sail

Heel — Foot of mast. A boat heels when it tilts sideways

Helm — Tiller or steering gear

Helm up or down — Moving tiller towards or away from the wind

Irons, in — Head to wind and unable to complete going about

Inboard — Within the boat

Isoclad — Trade name of a protective finish for polystyrene

Jib — Strictly speaking, one of the forward sails of a cutter, but commonly used for the single foresail of a sloop

Keel — The central bottom lengthwise member of the hull, or there may be twin or bilge keels

Kicking strap — Tackle or line from near the foot of the mast to the boom to hold it down

Knot — One nautical mile (6000 ft.) per hour

Leech (leach) — Aft edge of sail

Lee helm — Tendency of boat to turn away from the wind

Leeward — Toward the direction the wind is blowing

Leeway — Move sideways through the water

List — Tilt boat sidways

Lock — A water lift, using a gated chamber to raise or lower a boat

Luff — Leading edge of a sail

Luff, to — Bring a boat closer to the wind

Main sail — Largest or principal sail

Miss stays — Fail to go about

Neap tides — When the rise and fall of tide is least

Outboard — Outside the boat. An outboard motor cramps on the transom

Paddle — On a canal, the sliding door used to let water into or out of a lock

Painter — The rope attached to the bow of a dinghy for mooring

Pay off — Start sailing after being stationary into wind

Peak — Highest point of a gaff sail

Pinching — Attempting to sail too close to the wind

Pintle — The part of a rudder hanging with a pin

Polyfilla — Trade name of a stopping compound intended for household repairs, but which can be used to fill dents in polystyrene

Polyurethane — A synthetic paint finish

Port — The left side of a boat, when facing forward

Pound — A stretch of canal between locks

Quarter — Direction between astern and abeam. That corner of the transom

Reach — Sail with the wind abeam. A section of river between locks

Reef — Reduce the area of sail

Rowlocks — Metal fittings which take oars for rowing. Also called crutches

Rudder — The hinged fin used for steering

Run — Sail with the wind aft

Running rigging — All of the rigging which is adjustable and used to control sails

Scull — Propel a boat with a single oar over the stern

Sheet — Rope used to control a sail

Shroud — A side stay from the mast to the gunwale

Sloop — Single-masted craft with a main sail and one sail forward of the mast

Spinnaker — A light parachute-shaped sail used in light airs

Sprit sail — A four-sided sail with a spar (sprit) diagonally across it

Starboard — The right side of a boat when facing forward

Starboard tack — Sailing with the wind coming from the starboard side

Standing rigging — The permanent rigging supporting a mast

Stem — The extreme point of the bow

Stern — The aft part of the boat

Stern way (or board) — Sailing backwards, usually unintentionally

Tack — Sail a zig-zag course towards the wind. The lower forward corner of a sail

Thwart — Crosswise member, providing stiffness and forming a seat in a boat

Tide — Vertical movement of water due to gravitational attraction of sun and moon. Horizontal water movements associated with this are 'tidal streams'

Tiller — Handle used on rudder for steering

Transit — Two objects seen in line

Transom — The board across the end of a square-sterned boat

Trim — A boat is trimmed by moving the crew about. Sailes are trimmed by adjusting sheets

Under way — Moving through the water

Weather — The direction from which the wind is blowing

Weather helm — A tendency for the boat to turn into the wind if the tiller is released

Weir — A man-made waterfall, usually alongside a lock on a river

Windlass — The crank handle used to raise lock paddles

Windward — Towards the direction from which the wind is blowing

Yard — A spar supporting the top of a four-sided sail and crossing the mast

Yaw — Swing from side to side, particularly when running